ACCLAIM AND ACCOLA

"Kathleen Jamie's *Sightlines*, a collection of brilliant and enticing essays about natural phenomena, tingles with life. John Berger called her a 'sorceress,' and so she is."

—Diana Athill, **author of *Somewhere Towards the End***

"Kathleen Jamie has built a writing life around paying attention. The 14 personal essays in *Sightlines* include explorations—methodically reported and lyrically written—of secluded places like a cave in Spain whose walls are covered with prehistoric art, and the remote island of Rona in northern Scotland. In one brief, exquisite essay Jamie rescues a moth. And it's suspenseful."   —*The New York Times*

"Award-winning Scottish poet and essayist Jamie writes of her immersions in nature and history in 14 finely tooled, scrubbed, rinsed, and polished essays. . . . So fully does she give herself over to all that she witnesses, so unexpected are her perceptions, that Jamie's lustrous essays recharge our appreciation not only for the world's beauty and mystery but also for the gift poetic writers such as Jamie possess for translating sensory input into gloriously calibrated, revelatory language."   —*Booklist*

"This intelligent collection of 14 essays, informed by science and myth, heightened attention, and cultural dreams, is written with Scots brogue, language, and attitude that will give American readers a fresh view of nature."

—*Publishers Weekly*

"Kathleen Jamie's *Sightlines* dissects the natural world with precision, humor, and love. The essays in this book not only inspire us to look more closely, but also have the power to open us up to a new kind of emotional experience of the planet."
—*Orion* magazine editors, from the citation for the 2014 Orion Book Award for Nonfiction

"The dance of Jamie's words enacts the mind in motion as it moves between the shifting, shimmering processes of nature and art."   —*The Guardian*

"Jamie's prose is exquisite, yet never indulgent. . . . This is a book that will stay with you, as its sights and sounds have stayed with its writer."   —*The Sunday Telegraph*

"A haunting new collection from one of our finest nature writers. . . . Immensely beguiling. There are piquant descriptions that stop you in your tracks . . . but the real power of the writing derives from the steady increment of detail and the honesty of her responses to the natural world."
—*The Sunday Times* (London)

"Her written words make readers see with a clarity bestowed by only a few most gifted writers. . . . It is not often that the prose of a poet is as powerful as her verse, but Jamie's is. There are people uninterested in books about remote places and wild creatures; but to the rest of us [this book] will be a treasure."   —*Literary Review*

"There is such a precision, of both thinking and seeing, displayed in these works that you would have to be a very obtuse kind of reader not to realize that Jamie is a poet."
—*The Scotsman*

"At [one] point I put the book down again and thought: 'I wonder if I would actually kill to be able to write, or think, like that.' It's like this pretty much all the way through."
—Nicholas Lezard, *The Guardian*

SIGHTLINES

SIGHTLINES

KATHLEEN JAMIE

THE EXPERIMENT

NEW YORK

The Experiment, LLC
220 East 23rd Street, Suite 600
New York, NY 10010-4658
theexperimentpublishing.com

Sightlines was first published in the United Kingdom by Sort Of Books in 2012. First published in North America by The Experiment, LLC, in 2013.

THE EXPERIMENT and its colophon are registered trademarks of The Experiment, LLC. Many of the designations used by manufacturers and sellers to distinguish their products are claimed as trademarks. Where those designations appear in this book and The Experiment was aware of a trademark claim, the designations have been capitalized.

The Experiment's books are available at special discounts when purchased in bulk for premiums and sales promotions as well as for fundraising or educational use. For details, contact us at info@theexperimentpublishing.com.

Library of Congress Cataloging-in-Publication Data

Jamie, Kathleen, 1962–
  Sightlines : a conversation with the natural world / Kathleen Jamie.
    p. cm
  ISBN 978-1-61519-083-6 (pbk.) -- ISBN 978-1-61519-175-8 (ebook)
  1. Jamie, Kathleen, 1962---Travel--Scotland. 2. Jamie, Kathleen,
1962---Travel--Arctic regions. 3. Natural history--Scotland. 4. Natural
history--Arctic regions. 5. Scotland--Description and travel. 6. Arctic
regions--Description and travel. I. Title.
PR6060.A477S54 2013
914.11'0486--dc23

                              2013014023

ISBN 978-1-61519-083-6
Ebook ISBN 978-1-61519-175-8

Cover design and photo by Beth Bugler
Text design by Pauline Neuwirth, Neuwirth & Associates, Inc.

Manufactured in the United States of America

First printing September 2013
10   9   8   7   6   5

For the island-goers

CONTENTS

AURORA

———

THERE'S NO SWELL to speak of, just little lapping waves, so landing is just a matter of running the Zodiacs up onto the stony beach, allowing us to jump ashore. Not jump exactly: we swing our legs over the sides of the inflatable, and drop down onto the land, ideally between waves. You don't want to get your feet wet, because they'd soon freeze.

All along the shoreline lie trinkets of white ice, nudged up by the tide. A shore of ice and bones—people still come hunting here; the top of the beach is strewn with the bleached, butchered skulls and spines of narwhal and seal. Where the beach ends and the vegetation begins, an outboard engine lies abandoned, rusting violently.

While the Zodiacs are being secured, Polly and I take off our lifejackets and dump them beside the abandoned engine. Polly—I won't give her real name—is from central Europe, and is my cabin mate. I'm fortunate in her, enjoy her company. She speaks always with a sad or wistful laugh in her voice, or maybe it's just her accent.

We're part of a group who've chosen to leave the ship and come ashore, to walk up onto a low rocky ridge, for the sake of the view. Though 'view' is too benign a word for the vast, unnerving scale of this land, its clarity of light. I want to try to come to terms with where I am: a whole new world, a world with ice. We are in a bay; eastward, out on the open sea, icebergs are glowing a marshmallow pink in the morning sun. They've escaped the confines of the fjords and float free; the currents will bear them south toward their slow dissolution. Another iceberg, white and dazzling, guards the entrance to the bay where the ship is anchored.

Polly and I are both wearing old goose-down jackets—mine patched with gaffer tape—and hats, and gloves, and boots. When the party's assembled we begin trudging inland over crisp plants quite new to me. I've long loved the word 'tundra', with its suggestion of far-off northern emptiness, and I guess these must be tundra plants, under my feet. The plants are in their autumn colours, russets and fawns and mustard yellow. They spill between the rocks, dwarf willow and dwarf birch, and maybe bearberry. Among the trees' mazy horizontal branches grow lichens, and a kind of reed which curls at the end, like singed cat's whiskers. It's September. When we tread on the plants they release a dry herby smell into the crystalline air.

'Feather for you,' says Polly. Although I'd been looking down at the plants, it wasn't until I saw Polly bend and pick one up that I realised there were feathers scattered all over them. Goose feathers, caught on the dry leaves and twigs, frittering in the terse breeze. Droppings, too. The geese must have been gathered here so very recently, maybe only yesterday—hundreds of them, ready for the off. To my mind, geese only travel north, to some place beyond the horizon. But this is that place. From here, they go south. Involuntarily I look up and out to sea, where the icebergs shine, as if to catch sight of the last flight departing toward Iceland, toward Europe. But the sky is cold, blue and empty.

We cross the hummocky goose-plain, and begin the climb onto the ridge. There's about a dozen of us, from Europe and North America, tourists, still strangers to each other, beginning to get to know each other through polite conversation, getting to know the world a little, if that's what we're doing, such is our privilege. We've been instructed to 'stay behind the gun'. We have a guide, a young Danish biologist, who carries flares to scare them, and a rifle as last resort, in case of aggravated polar bears, but there are no polar bears. 'Polar bears?' one of the ship's Russian crewmen had shaken his head. 'Huh. They ate the last one years ago.'

With an outcrop of smooth bare rock to shelter us, we take off our rucksacks, set aside our cameras and the gun, crouch or sit down, out of the breeze. It's a stern breeze, blowing from the land, insouciant now, but, like everything here, it carries a sense of enormous strength withheld. Once everyone is settled, the guide makes a suggestion: why don't we keep silent, just for a few minutes, sit still and keep quiet, just listen?

We have the sea, deceptively calm and blue and serene with icebergs, stretching away eastward under an ashy sky. Below in the bay our ship rides at anchor, looking over-complicated among the smaller, white tufts of ice which drift soundlessly around it. Though white, the ship looks dirty, too, the way sheep suddenly look dirty when it snows. Behind the ship, the far side of the bay rises to a low brown ridge similar to this, and beyond that ridge is arranged a row of white pinnacles—the tips of icebergs grounded in a hidden inlet. Westward rises a range of brown jagged mountains, and beyond the coastal range there are hints and gleams of something I thought at first was a band of low cloud, but it's ice, maybe the edge of the inland icecap. The air is extraordinarily clear.

That's what we see. What we listen to, though, is silence. Slowly we enter the most extraordinary silence, a radiant silence. It radiates from the mountains, and the ice and the sky, a mineral silence which presses powerfully on our bodies, coming from very far off. It's deep and quite frightening, and makes my mind seem clamorous as a goose. I want to quell my mind, but I think it would take years. I glance at the others. Some people are looking out at the distant land and sea; others have their heads bowed, as if in church.

A minute passes, maybe two, maybe five, just the breeze and this powering silence—then a raven flies over. I knew Polly likes birds, so glance to see if she's noticed it and she has; her head is tilted back and quietly she's raised her gloved hand to shield her eyes. The bird, utterly black and alone in the sky, is heading inland on steady wings. It, too, keeps quiet.

They used to navigate by raven, the Vikings, there being no stars visible at such high latitudes in summer. The old sagas say that the Viking settlers of Iceland took ravens. Out of sight of land, wallowing at sea, they would release a raven and watch it climb the air until it was high enough to sight land. Where the raven headed, they followed in their open boats. Maybe ravens had brought them here, too, in their Greenlandic voyages, a thousand years ago. A thousand years. The blink of an eye.

Be quiet, I tell myself. Listen to the silence. I take my eye off the raven for a moment, and when I look back it's gone.

How long we sit there I don't know. I know only that I'd never heard anything like it, a silence that could dismiss a sound, as wind would dismiss a feather. Five minutes, ten, minutes in a lifetime.

Some people say you can never experience true silence, because you come to hear the high whine of your own nerves. That is to say, you hear the very nervous system which allows you to hear at all. Nerves because we are animals, not ice, not rock. Driven by cold and hunger. It's cold, our animal bodies say; best get moving. Keep warm, keep hunting. So, after maybe ten minutes, by some unspoken assent, a movement, a cough, our experience of deep silence is over, and life begins to whip us on our way. We all begin slowly to stand. Polly catches my eye, gives me the little smile and shrug which I already know are characteristic of her. We begin to move downhill, back toward the waiting boats. It's a while before anyone speaks.

———

Now it's mid-afternoon and hardly silence, there's too much excitement. We're back on the ship, we're underway and icebergs are coming. They appear ahead, one after the next, conveyed from a great manufactory, the distant

Daugaard-Jensen glacier at the top of the fjord. A dozen
of us, much the same dozen who had sat on the hill this
morning, are leaning out over the ship's white metal bow
as far as we dare, the photographers with their cameras,
the birders with binoculars, shouting above the wind and
engine drone. The wind is no joke; it would flay you alive,
a katabatic wind, they say, which flows downhill off the
icecap, and we're heading into it. You could go inside, of
course, and view the ice through glass, but what's the point
of that? You have to be out on deck, despite the cold, because of the cold, if you are to feel the white, deadening
presence of the icebergs. Someone calls, 'They're so . . . organic!' But organic is just what they're not. Their shapes
and forms are without purpose, adapted to no end. They are
huge and utterly meaningless.

The icebergs come on down the fjord in a slow caval-
cade, one by one, higher than the ship, closer and closer, and
every time I think 'Surely, surely, this time, we're going to
collide,' but always the ship turns aside gracefully, by just
a few degrees, and the iceberg glides away to port or star-
board. As they pass, they rear above like a building does,
all sculpted and white, with fissures of deepest blue, but
also they plunge on down underwater, in tilting levels of
sapphire, down into the mile-deep waters, where they have
their greater existence.

The fjord water is choppy and grey, and between icebergs
smaller morsels of ice bob along, now a rocking boat, now
an angel's wings. These little pieces look like Christmas
decorations but when the ship hits one it bangs like an oil
drum beaten with a stick. And there are the mountainsides,

the fjord walls. I realise I have the scale completely wrong; the scale is vast. On either side of the fjord, mountains rise to pinnacles of 6000 feet. They look as lifeless as cathedral spires, but I know now there are plants on their lower slopes, leading fugitive lives—animals, too. Small glaciers, some shrivelled far uphill, leave trails of moraine and gravel reaching down to the water. There's a lull, the wind, the engine, and then another iceberg appears, approaching with the hauteur of a huge catwalk model.

The next iceberg offers to the ship a ramp as smooth and angled as a ski jump. Just slide right up here, little ship, it seems to say, but the invitation is declined. It passes astern. Then the next appears down the fjord—a preposterous cake, with ink-blue shadows. Then another, the size of a three-storey house, with walls knapped into smooth, hard facets, like flint. Under the water's surface they are a blue you could fall into, as you could have fallen forever into the silence of the morning. It's like some slow delirium, a fantasy you can't shake, but with an undertow of menace. Although we shout when they appear, it's different when they glide past; no one speaks then. The cameras click, but the icebergs give nothing, suggest nothing but a white nihilism.

After a while the wind and cold become unbearable, so I leave the others out on deck and make my way along the port side, shoving open the heavy sea door under the lifeboat, into the blessed, slightly food-and-diesel-smelling warmth of the ship's interior. I shut the door; the wind stops. Then two flights of stairs take me up to the bridge. It's the same for all of us: we're like cats, always on the wrong side of every door, meeting each other always at the doors. Not everyone, the same dozen diehards: the huge German doctor with his huger camera, the Finnish birder, the Dutch photographer, Polly, myself. Desire to behold the icebergs, a fear we might miss something drives us out onto the deck, into the noise and scouring wind, until desire for a few moments' warmth drives us inside again.

On the bridge, a warm competent calm prevails. No one shouts there, certainly not the officers. Wide windows give panoramic views beyond the ship's mast and white prow of the fjord ahead, as the ship sails steadily on. It's a long fjord—the longest in the world—and we will keep sailing till nightfall. From here the icebergs ahead look like a jumbled barrier, as if there were no way through, but the radar shows otherwise. I like to look at the radar screen, and I like to watch the ship's captain and officers as they consult it.

The screen is the size of a small TV, and has shields around it the better to shut out any reflection or glare. On a black background, the fjord walls show as two green glowing lines, straight as the kerbs of a road; the icebergs are a rash of green dots between them. The officers move calmly between window and radar, radar and window, studying now one, now the other, checking one against the other, determining a course. In an alcove behind the bridge, screened at night by curtains, is the desk where the charts lie, with compasses and pencils, under an angle-poise lamp; a digital readout gives the ship's latitudes and longitude, as transmitted by satellite. It's quiet on the bridge, like a public library, but for the constant faint reassuring drone of the heating or ventilation.

But it's no good being indoors. Once warm again you have to be out—but the instant you put your shoulder to the seadoor, and lift your foot over the high step, so you are again under the lifeboats on their derricks, the wind claims you, you've to walk head down onto the bow, where the wall offers some little protection. Polly has been in for a coffee, but she, too, is back out again. She has been to these latitudes many times, but she's still keen, though, still interested. She is standing on a little metal step set into the bow.

'Like a harpoonist!' she calls.

'What's to harpoon? Any narwhal?' We'd love to see narwhal.

'No narwhal!' she replies, giving her little laugh.

We see few animals. There have been little ringed seals hauled out on small icefloes. They have happy-go-lucky expressions, despite their austere world, and they dive as the ship nears. And earlier—the Finnish birder was hopping across the icy deck in excitement—two white gyrfalcons appeared right overhead, attacking one of the young kittiwakes which have been the ship's constant companions. The falcons were working together. One (you could see the sandy bars of its undersides) tried driving the gull up from below, as the other descended toward her—there was a twist and turn of wings and a lot of shouted support—but the desperate gull was the more agile, and she managed to jink away into a lead of clear air, then fly up against the blue sky until she vanished, whereupon the falcons vanished, too. We look for birds and animals all the time, amongst the lifeless ice. I like the way the birds use the icebergs, how they perch on them, quite at ease, hitching a slow ride downstream. Glaucous gulls, a raven or two, another upright white gyrfalcon.

Another iceberg, and another. Some people say you can smell icebergs, that they smell like cucumbers. You can smell icebergs and hear your own nervous system. I don't know. Although they pass slowly and very close, I smell nothing but colossal, witless indifference.

———

Eventually, in the early evening, in a bay safe from icebergs, the anchor goes rattling down. Tufts and bows of white ice drift around the ship. The fjord is wider here, less relentlessly spectacular; there is a different geology. Instead of jagged basalt mountains, we look out on smooth hills of ice-worn rock, with patches of snow.

The wind has dropped, the water is tranquil enough to hold the hills' reflections. Soon it will be dark, but in the last of the daylight we watch—the photographers are all out on deck, their lenses trained—a family of seven stolid musk oxen as they trundle slowly over the hillside. The animals are much the same rusty colour as the vegetation they graze. With downward-curved horns framing their droopy faces, the males look like they're unhappily in drag. They all have a dusting of whitish guard hairs on their shoulders, like frost.

We eat and, as night falls, the waters of our anchorage change. I'm leaning over the side, puzzling about the sea 25 feet below. It's become a sluggish eerie green, and suddenly it reminds me of a horrible rubber sheet my mother used to produce, to complete our humiliation, if my sister or brother or I had a phase of bed-wetting. I haven't thought about that sheet for forty years, but here it is: deep in a fjord in east Greenland at nightfall, at 71 degrees of latitude, undulating around the ship: saltwater, slowly beginning to freeze.

Now it's after midnight, and dark. We have been to bed, lain in the dark in our cabins, but are up again, jackets and jerseys thrown over our pyjamas, boots, hats and gloves, and are again standing on the ship's foredeck, eight or ten of us, in twos or alone. Some lean on the rail, some stand in the middle of the deck. There is no electric light; the crew must have switched them off, so there is ship's equipment to negotiate in the darkness, winches and a mast. Although there is no wind now, it's deeply cold and we move with care, because the metal deck underfoot is glazed with ice. If we speak at all, it's in whispers.

The land is featureless now, and the water black, but the heavens are vivacious. We are standing with heads tilted back, marvelling.

Luminous green, teal green, the aurora borealis glows almost directly overhead. It intensifies against the starry night like breath on a mirror, and it moves. Across the whole sky from east to west, the green lights shift and alter. Now it's an emerald veil, now with a surge it remakes itself into a swizzle which reaches toward some far-away place in the east. We're like an audience—some gaze directly, others have again raised long-lensed cameras—standing in the deep cold, looking up, keeping silence, but it's not a show, it's more like watching fluidity of mind; an intellectualism, after the passivity of icebergs. Not the performance of a finished work but a redrafting and recalculating. In fact, because the aurora's green is exactly the same glowing green as the ship's radar screen, as the readout which gives the latitude and longitude, the aurora looks less like a natural phenomenon, more like a feat of technology.

Some people say you can hear the northern lights, that they whoosh or whistle. Silence, icebergs, musk oxen, and now the aurora borealis—the phenomena of the Arctic. This is why we've come here. This is why we are out on the freezing deck at midnight. The lights alter again. Low voices, the rapid clickering of cameras.

Polly comes up beside me and pokes me as best she can through all the layers of clothes. With head tilted back she whispers, 'They are changing without moving', which is true, and I fall to wondering if there are other ways of changing without moving. Growing older perhaps, as we are. Reforming one's attitudes, maybe.

Bright teal green. Once upon a time, whaling ships had come to these latitudes, with orders to return heavy with oil and baleen. Now the aurora alters into long trailing verticals, and it makes me think of baleen. Sifting. Sifting what? Stars, souls, particles. You could fancy the northern night were a great whale whose jaws our ship were entering.

We stand side by side watching, as the green lights close themselves in, then instantly flare out again like a concertina, like people can do who're really skilled at shuffling cards. It's a movement which ought to whoosh, but there is deep silence. There's something in the lights I recognise—a restlessness, a dissatisfaction with their own arrangements.

But: 'Where is everyone else?' I whisper. Aside from those few on the deck, the shapes of a few more people can be seen looking out from the windows of the bridge. The bridge, warm and reassuring with its competent officers and glowing green instruments. Where is everyone? My cabin mate clamps her arms to the sides of her goose-down jacket, stands rigid, and whispers in reply, 'Perhaps they are asleep.' She smiles as though she'd looked into the human condition some time ago, but has since moved on.

Or perhaps it is the cold. The cold is no joke. Stealthy, penetrating, already prospecting our bones. Perhaps they decided against heeding the impassioned calls on the PA to come and see the northern lights in all their spectacle, because of the cold. Perhaps they lie, as Polly suggests, like alabaster knights on a tomb, down in their cabins, changing without moving. Once more the lights alter and breathe. Someone gasps, then laughs softly and the cameras click.

Where, also, are the animals? The musk oxen and seals and gyrfalcons, and the kittiwake which escaped with its life—what do they do in the night, under the stars and the aurora? I like the aurora; there is something both elegant and driven in this green restlessness.

Once, I asked my friend John—half in jest—why we are so driven. By day John counsels drug addicts; by night he is a poet. He wrote back, half in jest: 'You know, my job isn't to provide answers, only more questions. Like: why are we not more driven? Consider: the atoms of you have been fizzing about for a bit less than five billion years, and for forty-odd of those years, they've been pretty well as self-aware as you. But soon enough they'll go fizzing off again into the grasses and whatever, and they'll never, ever know themselves as the sum of you again. That's it. And you ask me why we're driven? Why aren't more folk driven? Whatever are they thinking about?'

I have no idea what folk are thinking about. Right now, I'm thinking if we could taste the green aurora, it would fizz on the tongue and taste like crème de menthe. Right now, Polly and I are playing at finding the Pole Star, by means of the Great Bear. Just for fun, we won't have to navigate ourselves home like the old whalers by stars and sextants, or indeed by raven. We find the Pole Star and, with mock solemnity, salute it. It would show us the road north. There is always farther north. We see two shooting stars, and a satellite journeying on.

Now we are shrill with cold. Once again the flickering and pulsing of our own minds, our own mutability, tell us that's enough. Enough silence this morning, enough aurora now, thank you. Enough natural wonder, enthralling, mysterious and wild—we too are going to retire indoors.

———

Wakeful, Polly and I talk quietly in the dark. Curtains screen our bunks, so Polly is just a voice, a lilt and sad laugh. She's telling me that, some years ago, when she was about the age I am now, she suddenly fell ill. As a consequence, she suffered a calling into question, an inner rearrangement which was frightening, but liberating. As she speaks, I picture these events as happening in restless green, like the aurora borealis, in the dark of the mind, as revealing of the hidden as the radar screen. Or maybe it's like colliding with an iceberg, just as one is cruising along, in the middle of one's life. These things happen. You can look down and down into a beguiling blue and not know where you are. Polly still works the land, as she did before these events, growing food in good rich soil. She calls herself 'a peasant'. However, every year since that reassessment, she says, she has saved to make a journey such as this to the Arctic north, where there are no fruits and crops, only tundra and rock and ice.

'What brings you?' I ask.

'The birds bring me!' she laughs, and her accent makes it sound as though she travels in a chariot drawn by geese.

'I'm sorry you've missed the geese . . .' I say, and again comes that little laugh, out of the dark.

'But now they are in my fields!'

'And you?' she asks.

'Nothing like that,' I say, meaning, 'I have not been ill, not yet, or suffered a sudden calamity.'

'What brings me? I don't rightly know. But for thirty years I've been sitting on clifftops, looking at horizons. From Orkney, Shetland, St Kilda . . . ?'

'I know these places. And you wanted to know what was beyond?'

'No. Actually, I never did. Not until very recently. Suddenly I wanted to change my map. Something had played itself out. Something was changing.'

The northern lights may or may not make sound, but I believe they kept us awake. All that energy. In the morning, over breakfast, some people agree, but others scoff at this idea: they are eighty miles up—how can they keep you awake? They are just charged particles, trapped in the earth's magnetic field. True, but aren't we all?

We are tourists, on this trip, anyhow. Maybe also in the larger sense, John's sense. Here today, fizzing away into the grasses and silence tomorrow.

I'm not necessarily comfortable with having a place, a vast new landscape, mediated by guides, but it's how it is. I wouldn't last five minutes alone here, in the cold and the ice.

Among the passengers are doctors, dentists and engineers: people, it would seem, of professional certainty. People like myself—and Polly, I suspect—who don't quite know what we are. Who know only that we live short lives, that we float on the surface of a powerful silence, on the surface of a mile-deep fjord, with icebergs, that we're driven by some sort of life force, flickering and green.

I float on the surface of knowledge, too. Of climate science, for example. The icecap is two miles deep. In 2003, a team who'd spent seven years drilling through the Greenland ice to fetch up core samples at last hit bedrock. The ice at bottom of the core is 20,000 years old. They were bringing the deep past out of its silence, waking it up to ask it about change. There are people who crawl about on glaciers, measuring speeds and surges, and the calving of icebergs. Together they bring worrisome news from the farthest remotes. I sail on the surface of understanding, a flicker here, a silence there.

Abruptly, as though a door had slammed somewhere farther north, the weather changes. Cloud climbs low down the mountainsides and, suddenly, the following afternoon, it begins to snow and snow. Later the people of Ittoqqortoormiit—a small town of pitched roofed houses, where the sled dogs howl—will say that this year had been strange: no spring and no autumn, just bang! the brief summer, then bang! winter again. Maybe the geese had heard this change coming, under their clamour, through that appalling silence, and they'd chosen that moment to go. And the gyrfalcons. Maybe, the birders suggest, we are seeing so many gyrfalcons because they're arriving from yet farther north. If the snow falls and then freezes, say the naturalists, the musk oxen will starve.

We can't see the fjord walls, only cloud. Very soon, the ship's decks and rails and superstructure are under snow, the vessel becomes a frail, white-rigged thing, despite its metal and modernity and ice-strengthened hull. Not for the first time, as I move about the ship, I think about the nineteenth-century sailors, the whalers and explorers, the stories that come down to us, about how they got beset in the Arctic dark. When the snow lands on the water, it doesn't melt away. Instead it coheres into soft patches, little discrete clumps, until the water all around looks like an animal's pelt, lifting in the swell, breathing.

Looking down at the snow-covered water, I feel a sudden strong urge to be away from here, to head south. 'Like a goose!' I say to Polly.

She plucks at my old down jacket. 'It's because you are a goose!'

They take the ship down the fjord by night, negotiating icebergs through dark and snow. Tricky sailing, I shouldn't wonder, but the two officers of the watch, handsome if unsmiling, remain impassive as they work. Visibility is poor, but the aurora-green radar betrays the icebergs. The first officer leans over the radar, then moves back to the windows. I have no idea what he's thinking. From time to time he reaches overhead to a handle in the ceiling which controls a searchlight mounted outside on the deck above. As he turns the handle, a beam of light sweeps side to side beyond the ship's bows, picking out icebergs in the darkness ahead. As it moves through the dark, the searchlight beam glitters with falling snow.

After a long while watching from the bridge, I go outside, pushing through the doors and entering the sudden engine noise and cold. For once, I don't go to the front, but onto the aft-deck, where the Zodiacs are stowed under their winch. There is snow on the rails, snow underfoot. There is no sky, no stars, no aurora, only snow. The icebergs are much more sinister now. Each, in its weird majesty, slips alongside, lit white by the ship's lights, only to fall behind into darkness, into the ship's wake, reducing and reducing till it's nothing but a gleam, like the grin of the Cheshire Cat. I bear it as long as I can, then go back inside to the warm.

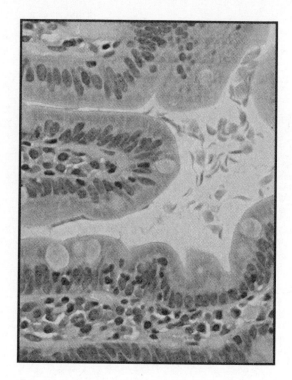

PATHOLOGIES

———

A FEW HOURS BEFORE my mother died, eventually of pneumonia, the disease they call 'the old man's friend', in a small side-room with muted lighting in our local hospital, there was a deluge of rain. I can't recall whether curtains or a blind screened the window, but I remember being puzzled by the sudden hissing noise, and crossing the room to peer outside, and the flat roofs, and the sheeting rain in the October night.

The sound of the rain, and of my mother's breathing. It was about 3 a.m. There would be no more medical interventions. Nature would be 'allowed to take its course'.

The days following such a death, when death is a release rather than a disaster, have a high, glassy feel, as though a note was being sung just too high to hear. It was a strange hiatus, all appointments cancelled. Between the death and funeral, the phone calls and the arrangements, between the time spent with my father and sister, and my brother's arrival home from abroad, I went out walking on the hills behind my town. The hillsides give views of the estuary below, then the land rising again on the river's north bank. The sky and river were beautiful, and glassy, as though they were the source of that high sung note. Nature was back in her accustomed place: outdoors, in the trees' colours, in the tidal flux of the river; in the fieldfares arriving to the fields. I often thought about the phrase 'letting nature take its course', how it sounded like a gallantry, how it suggested acceptance and timeliness.

About a month later, and farther north, there was a one-day conference, which was about humanity's relationship with other species. It was an impassioned affair. A government minister began the day, then a climate scientist gave dire warnings, then came writers and activists, all speaking with urgency about how we have to 'reconnect with nature'. We have a crisis because we have lost our ability to see the natural world, or find it meaningful. There had been a breakdown in reciprocity. Humanity had taken a wrong path, had become destructive and insulated.

The guests spoke from a raised podium with a nineteenth-century stained-glass window behind. Through the window, we, the audience, could see an occasional herring gull glide by, coloured red by the glass. A lunch of local venison was served, then came the afternoon speakers, who suggested that consumerism was a poor substitute for passion or wonder. One told a thrilling story about an encounter with sea-lions, another about a transforming experience with polar bears. It was dramatic in itself, but, he suggested, it carried wider meanings for our relationship with other creatures.

It was wearing on for Christmas. Outside the conference venue the streets were filled with shoppers, and the stained-glass window darkened early.

Perhaps I was still tired from my mother's death, thin-skinned and bad-tempered, but when the day ended with time for questions, I had some turning in my head, though I didn't raise my hand. About 'nature,' mostly, which we were exhorted to reconnect with. What was it, exactly, and where did it reside? I'd felt *something* at my mother's bed-side, almost an animal presence. Death is nature's sad neces-sity, but what when it comes for the children? What are vaccinations for, if not to make a formal disconnection from some of these wondrous other species? And what did we just eat, vegetarians aside? Deer meat, and very nice, too.

The train home was busy, and it broke down briefly, but people were cheerful, considering we were packed close to each other in a metal box on a Highland moor, but the last wolf was shot long ago.

In the New Year I wrote to Professor Frank Carey, Clinical Consultant in Pathology at Ninewells Hospital in Dundee. I'd met Frank before and knew him as a level-headed and considerate man, tall, with a soft Irish accent, and a good teacher. We were at a similar age and stage in life, with growing children and parents beginning to succumb. If he thought my request was prurient, he didn't say so. Rather he and his colleagues seemed glad of outside interest in their speciality. Usually people shy away.

I told Frank about the environmentalists' and writers'

conference, and how the foreshortened definition of 'nature' was troubling me. I'd come home grumpy, thinking, 'It's not all primroses and otters'. There's our own intimate, inner natural world, the body's weird shapes and forms, and sometimes they go awry. There are other species, not dolphins arching clear from the water, but the bacteria that can pull the rug from under us. I asked: please show me what's going on.

I was gabbling all this as we walked down the gleaming hospital corridors one February morning. Frank reached out to open yet another double door, saying, 'You know, till now, I'd never really thought of it as "nature".' I wondered, as I had at my mother's bedside, and the conference, if there was a distinction somewhere I had simply failed to understand.

―――――――

If pathologists are seen as slightly sinister, it's because they're the ones conducting dramatic post-mortems in TV detective shows. But the architecture doesn't help. The pathology labs were inevitably downstairs, in the lower reaches, the bowels of the building. Their main doors were protected by keypads, a sign announced fiercely that the department was 'under twenty-four-hour lock-down'. But I was there now. In his small office, Frank found a white lab coat for me, the first time I'd ever worn such a thing, the attire of the scientist, and he suggested we started with surgical specimens, in the 'cut-up room'. The cut-up room. I drew breath, but after my mother's death, and all the gentle euphemisms, and that conference, with its reverent talk of far-off polar bears and 'transforming experiences', I was actually quite glad to have arrived at a place where a spade was called a spade. Frank said, 'Are you squeamish?'

The door opened to a soft roar, the ventilation system. The wall opposite the door was all windows, but white blinds were drawn, and electric lights switched on. Tall shelving units held plastic trays and little tubs and boxes, and there were three or four long workbenches. At intervals on the workbenches lay green plastic chopping blocks. Other people, also in white coats, were already at work, standing at the benches, attending to things I couldn't see. I swore I would use no food similes, no culinary imagery at all, but of course it looked like a school cookery classroom, or 'domestic science', as they were pleased to call it then. The atmosphere was serious, but convivial.

Professor Carey led me to his place, then brought a tray of instruments. These he put to the left of the green board. To its right was a sink. In the tray were long tweezers and blunt-ended scissors. He spent a minute fixing a shining, newly sterilised blade onto a handle. Then he went off and at once returned with a grey plastic tub big enough to need carrying in both hands. He opened it and poured into a sink a gallon of liquid.

'Formaldehyde,' he said.

'It doesn't smell . . .'

'It's the ventilation. There's a very strong downdraught. Formaldehyde is pretty toxic, it wouldn't do to breathe it or get it on your skin.'

Then he grasped the object inside the tub and laid it on the block.

It was a drowned-looking thing, obviously of the body, big enough to be alarming: about ten inches long, rubbery brownish-pink, with an entourage of fattiness and membranes. I didn't know what I was looking at, but Frank soon told me it was someone's colon, or part of one— about a third. A colon is a tube, as you'd suppose, but the surgeon who'd removed it had sealed the lower end, the rectum end, with metal staples, and that end was about the size of a child's fist. The upper ten inches had been sliced open, so that part lay flat, revealing the inner surface. This surface was pale yellow-brown, and ribbed like a beach at low tide. It was a natural artefact alright, but far from elegant, and if I hadn't been told I couldn't have said whether it belonged to an aquarium, a puppet theatre or a bicycle repair shop.

'When was this taken out?'

Frank glanced at the notes. 'Two days ago.'

'So the patient is still upstairs?'

'She will be, yes. Oh yes.'

———————

Professor Carey began by turning the colon in his gloved hands, scrutinising and assessing it. He would have to write a 'macro-report', describing what he had, its dimensions and such, before it was sliced up. He stretched a piece of translucent membrane between three fingers to show me, and said complimentary things about the surgeon, a beautiful Iranian woman who was pointed out to me later, whose scalpel had carefully followed this membrane, releasing the colon from its context, bringing it to the outside world.

'The tumour's down here,' said Frank, pushing a gloved finger into the colon's lower end. He prodded around for a moment, then turned the colon inside out, to show me a hard whitish deposit adhering to the colon's inner wall. It seemed of no more consequence than chewing gum dropped on a pavement, but there it was.

The cutting followed a set procedure. Frank held the colon with one hand and with the long knife took parings from each end, the 'margins'. In due course these would be examined microscopically. If the tumour was cancerous, and cancer cells were found within a millimetre of the specimen's margins, there was a chance that cancer cells remained in the patient's body. These things determined the course of treatment prescribed. Then he sliced the tumour itself into pieces not much bigger than a thumbnail, and laid these in order at the top of his board. Then began the search for lymph nodes.

There's nothing dainty about the search for lymph nodes. If the cancer had spread from the original tumour, it would have done so via the lymph system. By examining these lymph nodes under the microscope, he would be able to tell if it had travelled and how far. Frank began carving decisively through the whole colon. As each slice slumped from his blade he dragged it to a clear section of the board and began mashing the fatty surround against the board with his fingertips. I watched as Frank worked, again trying to resist any food similes, but they would come. The pile of sliced colon mounting at the far edge of his board looked like chanterelle mushrooms, the fat squished under his fingers like cottage cheese. It might have been 'nature', but there was nothing uplifting about it. Well, we are predators and omnivores, we are meat and made of food, and the colon is part of how our animal bodies deal with food. At one point Frank said, 'Amazing how much like animals we are. This could be a pig's colon. We occasionally get veterinary specimens in, just for interest.'

'It shouldn't really surprise us . . .'

'That we're like animals? No, it shouldn't. But it still does.'

Lymph nodes feel like lentils or grains of rice; they resist being squashed. They are pale brown. As he found these auguries he laid them out in order. They looked like a row of baby teeth, only more yellow. One lymph node was markedly bigger than the others, which was not a good sign.

When he was satisfied, he tipped the board and scraped the residue of the colon into a polythene bag. The samples of margin and tumour and the lymph nodes went into tiny plastic boxes, ready to be mounted in wax, sliced, stained and prepared for the microscope. And that was that. One person's disaster, another's routine.

I kept having to do a mental exercise, every so often, to unhook myself from the colon being cut up in front of me, which was not a beautiful object of contemplation, and consider what it meant. To think upstairs, I mean, to that person lying ill and frightened and anxiously awaiting 'the results from the lab'. Other people in the room were working on lumps taken from breasts, an appendix. I'd said as much to Frank, about having to make an effort to empathise, and as he'd worked and I watched, we'd talked of people we knew who'd had cancer, even in our own families.

The sheer painful ghastly slog of it; the changed landscapes of a life, the unexpected declarations of love.

———————

A couple of weeks passed before I could again go the pathology labs; the snowdrops faded, the evening light lengthened. A neighbour had asked if we could look after her son for the day, while she went to the funeral of a young colleague who'd died of cancer. This time Professor Carey suggested we look at the next stage, the histology, or examination of cells through the microscope. Today it was a liver. The computer screen in his office was showing a substantial portion of one, with the gall bladder attached. The pictures had been taken after the liver was excised, but before cut-up. The severed edge, about three inches tall, had been cauterised and so was blackened slightly. Tiny threads hung down, where arteries had been tied off. They reminded me of climbers' gear, abandoned on a rock face. It had been removed, like the colon, because of a tumour—a big one, this time. The tumour bulged out of the liver like a gloved fist.

Professor Carey pointed out these features with his biro, then said, 'Okay. Tell me if you feel seasick'.

This time he meant seasick, not squeamish. The microscope was a double-headed one which allowed us both to see the same slide, and for one unused to microscopes it was like slipping into a dream. I was admitted to another world, where everything was pink. I was looking down from a great height upon a pink countryside, a landscape. There was an estuary, with a north bank and a south. In the estuary were wing-shaped river islands or sandbanks, as if it was low tide. It was astonishing, a map of the familiar; it was our local river, as seen by a hawk.

'It's like the Tay!' I said. 'At low tide. With the sandbanks.'

'I love the names of those sandbanks . . .' said Professor Carey. 'Now, we should start with the normal and move to the abnormal . . . let's look south.'

As though on a magic carpet, we flew to the south side of the estuary, and there Frank showed me how the arrangement of cells was ordered and calm. The sample had been stained with haematoxylin and eosin; organic, commonly used stains which show the nuclei and cytoplasm respectively. Frank could distinguish blues and purples; to my eye all was shades of pink, though I have a poor sense of colour. But it was a bright and pretty bird's-eye view of an ordered, if unusual land. I saw trails of nuclei, and the cells' supporting framework of reticulin. I could fancy the reticulin was old field dykes, the marks of a long inhabitation of the land. Here the cells were doing as nature intended, unconsciously getting on with tasks quotidian and wondrous: the filtering and clearing and storing and production.

'This is healthy tissue. Bear it in mind.'

Then we were swinging north, crossing the river, which was a vein rising into the liver from the intestine. On the river's north bank, we stopped and hovered over a different kind of place, densely packed, hugger-mugger, all dark dots that seemed too busy for comfort. Frank didn't have to tell me this was the tumour. Although it was also still, and fixed and a pretty colour, there was an unchancy, frenetic feel to it. There were too many nuclei crammed together and, as Frank pointed out, the 'architecture' was improper, the cells' structures and shapes were slewed, the supporting framework absent.

He said, 'The good thing is, these are still liver cells; they haven't been imported from a primary tumour somewhere else. They're still trying to behave like a liver, but . . .'

He looked quietly for a moment, then said, 'Cancer was named for the crab, because a cancer tumour sends claws out into the surrounding tissue. It's one thing we look for in arriving at a diagnosis of cancer: whether the tumour is self-contained, "encapsulated" or whether it's reaching out with claws. At cut-up I was happier, because it seemed self-contained, but look . . .'

We swooped low, till we were above a feature that crooked from the shore into the river, a bit like a jetty. When the magnification increased, you could see this was also crowded, and made of the same dense tumour tissue. 'And there is also this.' Now he focused on one of those areas I'd so delightedly thought of as sandbanks, with their old, suddenly apposite Scots names: the Reckit Lady, the Shair as Daith. There, too, we looked down on the same kind of tissue.

'So we have some vascular invasion'.

Frank made a note, then said, 'We had a trainee for a while, and whenever she saw something like this, she'd say, "Aw, what a shame. What a *shame*." Now, let me show you something else.'

It all seemed like bad news but I leaned back into the microscope, to be guided by Frank's trained eye. In the healthy liver, he led me to two tiny dots and increased the magnification. The dots expanded into a double image, what looked like a pair of boxing hares.

'That's a cell dividing normally. The chromosomes lined up equally. That cell has been arrested just at that moment in its cycle; this is life. But see here.'

Again we travelled north, over to the tumour, and within its mass Frank found what he wanted at once. It was another dividing cell, but if they were two boxing hares, one hare was hugely bigger than the other, claiming strength and advantage. His report would call them 'abnormal mitotic figures'—cells dividing wrongly, and too many, and too fast.

I sat back and rubbed my eyes.

'So that's that?' I asked bleakly, meaning, 'That's going to kill him?' The little hook out into the vein, the intimate, crowded island, a mere smear on a glass slide.

Frank sounded surprised. 'Not at all! He's in with a good chance. The tumour's been successfully removed, and you can't actually make definite predictions from what we've seen . . . He'll have chemotherapy. And the liver regenerates, you know. Though he's had that large section removed, it'll be growing back.'

As Frank put the slides away on a tray in their proper order I glanced about his office, resting my eyes. A couple of lab coats on a peg, books and files on a shelf, pathology textbooks, a child's drawing, a bicycle helmet, the window screened by a pale blind. 'Flying' may have been an illusion, but it was one my body believed, because I was feeling queasy, with all this swooping down and up. Queasy, but cheered.

'Would you like to see more? You said you were interested in infections. I set aside a couple of infections for you . . .'

'You're very kind.'

This time the country beneath was a gorgeous sapphire blue. It had a north-facing shoreline and, a mile or so inland, so to speak, were regularly spaced ovals, end-on to the coast, that might be craters, or even sports stadiums. Frank was describing it to me with his customary quiet level-headedness. He was speaking of 'columnar structures' but it took me a while to understand that he meant the ovals; they were sections cut horizontally through columns. These were acid-producing glands; we were in the lining of someone's stomach.

Between the oval structures were valleys, if you like, fanning down to the shore. Frank wanted to show me something in one of these valleys and I couldn't find it at first; it took several patient attempts—this microscope didn't have a cursor device to point at things. It was a very human moment, a collusion of landscape and language when one person tries to guide the other's gaze across a vista. What vistas I'd seen. River deltas and marshes, peninsulas and atolls. The unseen landscapes within. You might imagine you were privy to the secret of the universe, some mystical union between body and earth, but I dare say it's to do with our eyes. Hunter-gatherers that we are, adapted to look out over savannahs, into valleys from hillsides. Scale up the absurdly small until it looks like landscape, then we can do business.

'There!' said Frank. 'Isn't that a pastoral scene? They're grazing!'

I had it: six or seven very dark oval dots, still tiny, despite the magnification, were ranged across the blue valley, like musk oxen on tundra, seen from far above.

'This is *Helicobacter pylori*—they're bacteria. They irritate the stomach, the stomach produces too much acid, and so they cause stomach ulcers. Obvious as anything now, but they just weren't seen till 1984. It was an Australian pathologist who spotted the association between inflamed stomachs and these things. He was a bit of a crazy. No one took him seriously, no one believed stomach ulcers could be caused by bacteria. But . . . he found another crazy to work with and together they got the Nobel prize. Probably saved thousands and thousands of lives. The thing is, you perceive what you expect, what you're accustomed to. Sometimes it needs a fresh eye, or a looser mind . . .'

'You can die of stomach ulcers?'

'Yes. You bleed.'

'Grazing' was the word. Although the landscape was bright blue—a stain called *Giemsa*, it was an image you might find in a Sunday-night wildlife documentary. Pastoral, but wild, too. So close to home, but people had landed on the moon before these things were discovered, free in the wilderness of our stomachs.

'You wonder what their function is, their purpose . . .'

'No purpose. They're not conscious. They just are. These things have been co-evolving with us, for millennia and millennia. They've adapted to live in acid. There are some people, you know, who take the stomach as evidence of 'intelligent design', because it contains its own acid; you walk around with a bag of acid in you, and come to no harm. But it's evolved that way, and these things have evolved with it.'

'So what will happen?'

'A course of antibiotics should put paid to them.'

'And do you think there are other things, other associations, we're just not seeing?'

'Oh, certainly. Now, would you like to look at something else?'

Of course I did. More little journeys to strange new shores. The nature within. Nature we'd rather do without. If I were a pathologist, I think I ought always to have that woman in the room, the one who kept saying, 'Aw, what a *shame*', a one-woman Greek chorus; otherwise I fear I'd be seduced by the bright lights and jewel colours, the topography, flora and fauna, so caught up among the remote and neutral causes I'd forget the effects.

Again Frank swapped slides, and again the world was pink. We were in the small intestine and this time I had no trouble seeing the beast in question; it was cruising along the indentations of a coastline like a gunship. A pink triangular balloon, with a thin mean tail—though microscopic, it was big enough to be thuggish, and I said so.

'Ah, you see, you're personalising it. It's just a one-celled organism, a protozoan.'

'Morally neutral.'

'Morally neutral. This is *Giardia*. You've been to Asia . . . you know, stomach cramps, constant diarrhoea? So debilitating. And chronic. It doesn't kill you, but it makes you very ill . . . it's endemic in Asia and Africa, but occasionally it turns up here, in wells and springs. Cattle get it too, and sheep and deer.'

He studied it for a moment, then leaned back from the microscope, saying with sudden feeling, 'This thing's a *pest*.'

Pestilence and disease. It's pretty grim. Who wants the privacy of their body invaded and bits cut out and chopped up and the remnants scraped into a polythene bag? But we'll go a long way not to die. Who wants their neighbour down the street or round the world to bleed into her stomach when a course of antibiotics will do the trick? We need disease to dance us on our way; we need to halt it if we're to live morally. Twin truths, like boxing hares.

I drove home along the river I'd fancied I'd seen in the poor man's liver cells. The tide was in, no sandbanks. The inner body, plumbing and landscapes and bacteria. The outer world also had flown open like a door, and I wondered as I drove, and I wonder still, what is it that we're *just not seeing*?

———

On my third visit Frank relayed an unsettling invitation. A colleague, Professor Stewart Fleming, whom I had met last time, was that morning conducting a post-mortem.

We looked at each other.

'Think about it,' said Frank. I paused for a long moment, then asked: 'What do you think yourself?'

It was his turn to pause. 'Why don't we look in later, in a couple of hours, when he's finishing up, just for a minute or two?'

It lay on my mind. Why refuse? Because it felt scary, and like a transgression. My own motives may be impure: idle curiosity, a good dinner-party story—guess what I did on Wednesday! Why attend? Because . . . there were just some things to come to terms with.

A featureless door, guarded by a keypad. No signs, no notices declaring lock-downs, just a door in the wall. As Frank was tapping in the number, my heart lurched in fear of what it would open to reveal.

'What are we going into?'

'Sorry,' said Frank. 'Nothing, here.'

A narrow flight of stairs, leading (of course) down, and round a corner. At the bottom was another door. This one gave into a small hall, lined with white locker doors, with people's names handwritten in red pen. Corpses, waiting for the undertakers to arrive and, discreetly, take them away. A porter gave us a jolly hello as we passed and at a further corner Frank did hold out a staying hand, saying, 'Wait here a moment', as he went ahead.

No doubt they were doing some tidying. Concealing this and washing that. I had no lab coat today, and felt suddenly wrongly dressed: it had all gone serious and I was in too bright a skirt, too casual a top. Everything around was clean and metallic. Then Frank reappeared, saying, 'You can come in now.'

The scene was composed like a painting, or a ritual: the living, and the concealed dead. In a wide, clean open space the body, shrouded in white, lay on a metal table to the left. At the back wall a figure in green gown and hat glanced toward us, then turned back to the sink where she was occupied. Above her were windows, for observers. Professor Fleming, dressed in green scrubs, was pushing toward me a metal tray on wheels. I couldn't see what lay on the tray until we met, and I looked down. At that point he said, 'Okay?' I think he meant, you're not about to faint? It happens, sometimes.

'Okay,' I said.

He pointed. 'This is the heart, this is the left lung.' With splayed fingers and a soft scraping motion, he pulled the heart across the tray. It left a smear of blood. 'I've cut it open, see?' Deftly—this was a substance he was used to handling—he began to fold the opened heart back into shape, like a small bag. The word 'cutpurse' came to my mind, an old name for a thief. I nodded, and, though I would have liked to have seen again how the heart was made, more slowly, it seemed improper to ask and already I was aware of the smell, fresh, rude, rising up and summoning some primal response I didn't really want to acknowledge.

I looked from the heart, the chubby texture of its walls, its inertness, up to Prof Fleming's eyes as he spoke, back down to the heart. The quick and the dead. I could sense, rather than see, the shrouded shape of the dead man.

The lung, smaller than you might imagine, had a smoother texture, but worked through its redness were threads of black.

'That's just carbon deposit. Every city-dweller has that in their lungs . . .'

Now the smell was insistent, a blood-red rose.

'And what . . . ?' I asked.

'This . . . You'll have heard of thrombosis?' He pointed to a dark gobbet on the cut-open heart.

'That's a thrombosis, in the right atrium. Also the heart's enlarged, 630 grammes, a good third bigger than you'd expect for a man of this size. He had a condition that made him susceptible to this . . .'

I thought 'we are just meat', then called it back. Flesh, bodily substance, colons and livers and hearts, had taken on a new wonder. If you had to design a pump or gas-exchange system or device for absorbing nutrients, you would never, ever, think of using meat.

'And his wife asked for a post-mortem. She wanted to know the cause of death. Although he'd been ill a long time, his death was very sudden. She had looked after him. She wants to know if there was anything else she could have done . . .'

The cold organs laid on the cold tray. They didn't call out, didn't suggest any great meanings; they were plain and soft and vulnerable, with their billowing smell of meat. After this one last favour, granting absolution to the man's wife, they'd be returned to the body for cremation or burial, returned to the elements.

We all nodded. Enough.

'Are you hungry?' asked Frank. 'Let's go and get a sandwich. That's the tradition.'

———

'The natural evidence of our mortality,' Professor Fleming called it. Hearts and lungs, a colon that could be a pig's. That's the deal: if we are to be alive and available for joy and discovery, then it's as an animal body, available for cancer and infection and pain. Not a deal anyone remembers having struck—we just got here—but it's not as though we don't negotiate.

In the staff common room there were low upholstered benches and a water cooler. The windows gave views of car parks and newly built houses beyond. A leaf, swirled up in the breeze, flattened itself against the window, a gull wheeled in the air. God knows, someone has to plead for the non-human, and cry halt to our rapacity, like the speakers at the conference, even if he has antibiotics and antiseptics in his rucksack. Or maybe that's the beginning of a truce.

The doctors' conversation soon turned to hospital politics and the dread hand of management. Enough, indeed. Enough bodily marvels for one day. I left them to their work just as visiting hour was beginning, and the foyer filled with people. That heart smell haunted me: for a while it was unshakable, as though, like a wolf, I could sense it everywhere; in the old and middle-aged and babes in arms, all seeking their way towards their relatives and friends. It felt surprisingly good to be part of that rough tribe of the mortal, and good to be well, able to stride outside again, back into the cool March breeze.

THE WOMAN IN THE FIELD

———

BECAUSE OF THE EARTHFAST NOTION that time is deep, that memories are buried, the Neolithic and Bronze Age artefacts occupy the windowless basement level of the National Museum. To visit the prehistoric, one must descend turnpike stairs, or travel down in a lift—either way, down—until the pressure of the building, of thousands of years of subsequent history, is piled on top.

Down there, a diorama shows how the land was then. Two stuffed wolves slink through a forest, pursuing a wild boar. A tape plays wolf-howls and the yaffle of a woodpecker. Opposite that, mounted in a glass box, is the massive bovine skull of the now extinct aurochs. It looks like something cast in a foundry, like it ought to belong upstairs, under 'Industrial Revolution'. This skull was found, as it happens, in the small town where I now live, with its single main street and primary school, and where, last year, a log boat was carefully pulled out of the river mud, where it had lain since the Bronze Age.

I'd come to the museum to visit something in particular, but I'm distracted; first by the wolves and aurochs, and now by a gleaming bronze dagger with a pommel of whalebone, which the label says is a replica of one found in a bog. It shows how new and desirable such objects were, before they spent four thousand years corroding in the earth. But at last I find what I'm looking for.

It's a clay bowl, that's all; what the archaeologists, with imaginative flair, call a 'food vessel'. It's displayed in a tall glass case with a number of other bowls small and large, artfully arranged on glass shelves. A load of old pots, the epitome of museum dullness, unless you like that sort of thing.

The bowl I want to see has been placed together with another at the front of the case slightly apart from the rest, as though these two had things to discuss, which they well might. They are both reddish brown, and about seven inches tall, though one is fatter than the other. The fatter one is a bit lopsided, so it inclines toward its neighbour. Both are decorated all over with bands of grooves and half-moon-shaped jabs and it's this—the near-matching decoration—which announces them as siblings. It's remarkable, but though they're nigh on 4000 years old and were discovered a century apart in different corners of the country, these two Bronze Age bowls were almost certainly made by the same potter. One was discovered on the south banks of the Forth, the other farther north in Perthshire, in a place close to the River Earn. Those places ('findspots,' the archaeologists say) are only twenty miles apart as the crow flies, but the vessels must have been transported to their destinations, possibly from the potter's workshop in a third place, by a route much longer on the ground. They must have been taken by boat through a complex of rivers, or been carried on foot over hill-passes and through wooded valleys, where wolves may well have pursued the wild boar.

They had lain a long time in the earth, but both are clean now in their glass case, and contain nothing but shadows. If they were indeed the work of a craft potter, they might have been fired to order, perhaps at the behest of a messenger. So, despite difficulties, people and news and goods must have spread through the country more quickly than we might suppose.

I was a teenager when I first became aware of the past, manifest as relics in the land. A teenage antiquarian, thrilled by standing stones, tumuli, ley lines and all that; what their aficionados grandly called 'earth mysteries'. Questing after a well or earthworks was what got me out of my parents' overheated living room and off into the local byways and hills. I had a duffel coat, suede boots and flared jeans that soaked up the wet; hopeless attire, but near to our modern housing scheme on the outskirts of the city were the remnants of two, three, five thousand years of occupation. I cycled to visit a long-barrow, which is now a roundabout at a motorway intersection near the airport; I hiked up onto the Pentland hills to examine a few ditches and banks which the map announced as an 'earthworks', and one Boxing Day, just to get out of the house, I walked miles to visit a stone pocked with cup-marks. It stood where it had been raised thousands of years before but an estate of 1930s bungalows swirled around it now. It was snowing lightly. What I saw wasn't a standing stone overwhelmed by bungalows but, rather, I fancied I could feel the pulse of ancient energy in the land, quietly persistent even in the slushy suburban sprawl.

Then, one day in May 1979, it may even have been my seventeenth birthday, I sat my last, lacklustre exam and left school without ceremony or much notion of a personal future. A day or two later, my mother drove me the thirty miles from our house into rural Perthshire. She had suggested librarianship, which was the stock idea for a kid who read books. I did read books: the paperback stuffed into my haversack on the back seat was by Tom Wolfe—*The Electric Kool-Aid Acid Test*. She suggested secretarial college. When she said these things, tears of belligerent dismay pricked at my eyes. No one suggested university.

The route we followed in the family VW Passat was almost the same, I now realise, to that which separates the sites where the two decorated food vessels were found. We, too, travelled by river valley and hill-pass. We followed the motorway upriver to Stirling, skirted the edge of the Ochil Hills, dipped into Strathallan and crossed the Allan Water, and continued through farmland and old villages. It was an alien land. We drove narrow roads shaded by huge trees, passing the driveways and gates to secluded private houses larger than either of us had ever entered. Blue election posters were still nailed to roadside trees, but they would soon be removed. They'd done their work—ten days before, Margaret Thatcher had been voted into office.

There must have been an exchange of letters and directions. I must have seen an advert recruiting volunteers, applied, and been told to turn up at this mid-May date. I remember nothing of that except that I had to bring a trowel, 'cast not welded'. I had no idea what that meant, except that it seemed suggestive of the ancient magic of metalwork. It meant only that cast trowels were stronger, and there would be a lot of trowel work.

We crossed the Earn by a lovely old four-arched bridge, then took the right turn under a road lined with tall pines. On the right, the river; on the left, after half a mile, an unremarkable farm track began. We turned in, the track at once sloped uphill, and led quickly onto a level terrace of farmland. Suddenly, when we crested the rise, there appeared the long ridge of the Ochils, five miles away and blocking any view further south. This low but determined range of hills formed the entire horizon. To the north, more hills, higher and jagged, the beginning of the Highlands. All of this—the crossing of rivers, the terrace of land, the encircling raised horizon was relevant, but I didn't know it then.

We'd arrived at something which seemed part wartime billet, part hippy commune, and no one was around. The track led to the back yard of a substantial old-fashioned farmhouse, derelict-looking but obviously in use. It was L-shaped, built of grey stone, with pitched roofs. At its eastern gable stood a few trees. At its west side, an arched barn. A couple of caravans were parked up nearby, and a lived-in ex-army ambulance painted yellow, with a stovepipe emerging from its roof. A field away, beyond a line of sycamores, were low heaps of freshly dug earth.

The farmhouse door was open, but a deep puddle had formed at the threshold, and hessian sandbags were piled up to keep the water out of the house. We negotiated the puddle and entered a dim kitchen with a long table flanked by benches and a sink in the window. A woman dressed in shorts and a T-shirt was stirring a pot. She turned and gave me and my mother a cursory look. To me she seemed old, and senior—twenty-eight or so. I explained myself, but didn't understand at first when she spoke; many of the people here were itinerants with accents I'd simply never heard before, not for real: London or Devonian, or, like this woman, a clipped, old-fashioned English public school. My mother said, brightly, 'Don't worry, I'm not staying!' She didn't, either.

What was being excavated was a 'henge'. Henge, hinge, to hang—the word first applied to Stonehenge, with its great stone lintels, had come to mean any Neolithic circular enclosure, which is to say a circle of standing stones or wooden posts, with a surrounding ditch and possibly a bank. Spanning the ditch, which can be deep, there may be one or two causeway entrances. Henges are not uncommon, but their purpose is still obscure, and might always be. They attract baggy words like 'ritual' or 'ceremonial'. Some, like Stonehenge, are orientated toward solar or lunar events, but thirty years ago that was still a moot point.

This one, on a farm called North Mains, had been discovered—or rediscovered—from the air. Two years before, in 1977, the Royal Commission on Ancient and

Historical Monuments had conducted an aerial survey of the whole country. When Antoine de St-Exupéry said, with typical hauteur, 'the aeroplane has unveiled for us the true face of the earth', he meant the vastnesses of the Sahara, the rippling oceans he saw beneath him, against which human habitation was a paltry thing. But it's true of human traces, too—the small and lost and intimate are also revealed. Prehistoric sites, invisible to a walker on the ground, can show from high above.

'Crop mark' is the phrase. On the black-and-white photo this henge had shown up as thick dark circle, which the field wore like a tattoo. And, like living memories, crop marks are fickle: they respond to different weathers and seasons. One stalk of corn will grow taller than another a yard away, because of ancient disturbance to the ground in which it was sown. It knows a secret, which everyone else has forgotten, and which it discloses to the sky.

My own memory of that summer is patchy now, inevitably. Some images, a 'taste', some names, a feeling of being much out in the sun and wind, and of being caught up with new excitements and possibilities.

The site was already well under way. It was an orderly place of scraped earth and excavated holes and spoil heaps. It lay beyond the sycamores, five hundred yards away from the farmhouse, on the same flat terrace, near the lip of a defile that fell away sharply down to a meandering tree-lined burn. There was the River Earn on one side of this raised terrace, and a burn, the Machany Water, winding along on the other, and, farther in the distance, that wall of hills. Due east lay the farmlands and wooded slopes of Strathearn, the long fertile river valley that became, eventually, the Firth of Tay, and the North Sea.

We worked by day, but the long midsummer evenings were our own; we were free to linger outdoors in the cool gloamings, at leisure until work began again in the morning. About twenty of us dossed down in the farmhouse at night, and every morning we filed out onto site. I loved it.

The exams I'd just taken were already far from my mind. The Stone Age was closer to me than secretarial college ever would be.

May was cold and blustery and often we were rained off, and obliged to sit in the wooden site huts—a couple of big garden sheds—drinking tea, smoking roll-ups, watching the rain slant across the door. At day's end, dusty and weary, we trooped back to the farmhouse. Every day, on a rota, two people quit work mid-afternoon and retired to the farmhouse kitchen to assist on a marathon of cooking. What did we eat? Who did the shopping? I couldn't say.

The farmhouse was due to be demolished. That's what we heard. It had obviously been empty a while, but there were many derelict farm buildings then. People were still leaving the land; there was as yet no appetite for renovating old mills and steadings and the like. In short, there was no great need to take care of the house; this youthful invasion was its last hurrah. If there were what estate agents call 'original features'—fireplaces, shutters, panelled doors, I was oblivious to them. There was a lot of brown varnish and the floors were bare, good for sleeping and dancing.

In every room—five, I think—were rough furnishings: old mattresses, rucksacks and sleeping bags. Of the two large public rooms downstairs, one had been commandeered by more longstanding volunteers, the weather-beaten old hippy element. They had installed a couple of old car seats.

One of the inhabitants was a long-haired man we called Pete the Lech. He did to me as he did to all the girls: sidled up while my back was turned, slunk his arms around me and asked, huskily, if I'd sleep with him. I remember the texture of his hair on my face and the smell of patchouli as, laughing, I said, 'No'. 'Fair enough,' he said and wandered off. By then I'd read enough of *The Electric Kool-Aid Acid Test* to recognise the quotation painted gleefully on his door. It was Ken Kesey's great scrambled pun, 'No left turn unstoned.'

There must have been a bathroom, some means of washing, an outside toilet even, for the twenty-odd 'diggers' billeted in the house, but that's another nicety I can't recall. The tribal elders, our bosses, were in their late twenties. Everyone was young. It's a wonder to me now how people so young could carry all this. As in wartime. As in the Neolithic.

No stone was left unturned. That was the day job. There was a Neolithic monument, it had lain in the earth for four thousand years, and our task was its swift and meticulous destruction. The site, the henge, was subdivided into four areas, each area the responsibility of one archaeologist, all of whom reported to the overall director, Gordon Barclay.

These real archaeologists were remote figures who lived aside in caravans, who told us what to do, and who hauled us back to work when the rain showers passed.

Mostly I worked within the inner sanctum, an area about twenty-five metres in diameter, and was engaged in 'stripping down'—that is, carefully and, with the trowel, scraping away just a centimetre's depth of the hard-packed subsoil which formed the interior of the enclosure. Several of us did this job. Hair in my face, knees on the ground, I held my new cast trowel and scraped at the earth. Had they still existed, we'd have been within a circle of twenty-four wooden posts, possibly with a wattle fence strung between them. Immediately outside the ring of posts, there would have been a ditch almost three metres deep, like a dry moat, and then encircling that, a raised bank, six foot high in its day. Such had been the original, Neolithic construction. Every day some diggers were seconded into the outer ditch, to empty it of long centuries of infill. I didn't envy them, stuck down a hole all day. All the post-holes and the ends of the ditch were emptied, and the fill carried away in wheelbarrows to the spoil heaps. I still loathe wheelbarrows.

So this was what we did: kneel over a portion of earth, a metre square or so, and scrape with the trowel's edge, trying to apply the weight evenly, so as not to score or scratch, or make one side tilt lower than the other. Some diggers were better at this than others. Although the word 'diggers' still carried a whiff of the radical English movement, the seventeenth-century communitarians, and they were often ragged and long-haired, there was, even amongst them, a hierarchy. A sign of experience was a trowel worn away to a thin dagger-like blade. With this one tool, it was possible to spend half the year in a journeyman or gypsy way, hitch-hiking from site to site, working a few weeks here and there. In the right hands it was a sensitive tool—you learned to feel, or hear, the grind of an earth-hidden stone or pottery shard before you saw it. Sometimes a little pebble tumbled away as the trowel edge passed over it, but a larger stone, as yet hidden, just beginning to emerge, sent a tiny seismic thrill along your arm. This was what you wanted, the excitement of a 'feature'.

We can talk a great deal about post-holes and ditches, but what actually happened at that place so long ago, at what time of year, and who travelled how far to attend, and what they called the place, and whether they came by boat or on foot, and if there was a distinction between those deemed fit to enter the inner enclosure where we worked, and those who, like a crowd outside a cathedral, were obliged to stand at a remove, we have little way of knowing, though some bold theories are emerging. You can't help but suspect social distinctions have been with us for a very a long time.

Over the last week of May the ditches were excavated, the post-holes within the ditch all emptied out, measured, photographed and the enclosed area carefully scraped down. You could tell where a hole had been dug 4000 years ago, and a wooden post put in, by a change in colour and texture of the soil. You could tell that the posts had, over the course of the years, simply rotted away. They had not been set ablaze in a great spectacle, as had apparently happened at other henges. People bent over their patch of soil, squinted through theodolites, drew on paper pinned to boards, and for this were paid a few pounds a week pocket money, fed, given a space on a floor. For a while it felt like a life. It was rough and ready, but with more purpose than a commune and too short-lived for much tension to build.

Mostly, we were just clearing, but the work had its own satisfactions. It was hand work, nitty-gritty. I liked the bite on the point of the trowel as it scraped back a layer of soil, the feel of earth. For long moments, though, I thought of nothing but tea break, and discomfort, the nuisance of having my hair blow over my face. But at other times you could lose yourself in that minuscule landscape, a tiny Sahara seen from miles high. It often surprised me, when I leaned up to rest my back, that I was in a field in Perthshire. I liked to see the unchanging, stalwart ridge of hills, to be reminded of the wider landscape, of which we, bent over our trowels, seemed to be the centre—possibly with reason. I mean, there was a reason these 'ceremonial enclosures' were constructed where they were. Prehistoric people may not have had aeroplanes to reveal the face of the earth to them, but they could certainly read a landscape.

———————

A few photos: one shows a dozen diggers sitting on the ground, legs outstretched, backs against the wooden wall of a site hut. A sunny, blustery day, but cool, judging by the jackets and windblown hair and the squinting into the sun. Everyone is under thirty, and everyone has a mug; we are engaged in the ritual/ceremonial of the tea break. Five more minutes and we'd be summoned back to work.

Another shows a young man standing down in a ditch, for scale. He is friendly-looking, thin and red-haired. I forget his name. The end wall of the ditch is a third taller than he is, maybe nine foot.

In that ditch it was possible to tell where, one day four thousand years ago, one labourer had finished his shift and another had taken over. *Plus ça change.* When he'd climbed out, he'd have seen the same ridge of hills as we did, the same long river valley, with woods and clearings. He'd have gone off, maybe down to the burn to wash away the grime, to take a drink, maybe to lie looking up at the clouds before he had his meal.

The director in his report calculated that a hundred people would have been required to build the henge, probably organised in gangs. A similar team, organised in gangs over two seasons, dismantled it again.

A third photo shows four diggers in the golden evening light, outside the farmhouse. They are dancing. Their shadows are long, and reach right across the yard.

———————

It was because of the Avro Lancaster that the henge had to be excavated. That was what we heard. The site was being dug because the landowner, Sir William Roberts, intended to extend a runway over the top of it, because of his Lancaster.

Westward of our site, still on the same level of land, were couple of large hangars, a grass landing strip and a windsock. They constituted the Strathallan Aircraft Museum, a private collection of mostly WW2 aircraft. It was open to the public and, in the hangars, amongst other things, were two Spitfires, a De Havilland Mosquito, a Lysander and a Hawker Hurricane. The Hurricane still flew, and often passed above our heads as we worked. It came low over the henge, over the perimeter fence, to land and taxi to a standstill down at the hangars. We grew accustomed to the sweet snarl of its engine. It was a wartime sound, as evocative as the wail of an air-raid siren. But now—this is what we understood—Sir William had acquired a Lancaster.

What can we say of the Lancaster? Some reckon it a most beautiful aircraft. The most beautiful-sounding. The little Battle of Britain Hurricane had but one Rolls-Royce Merlin V2 engine. Lancasters had four, wing-mounted, 1400 horsepower. At about 40,000 lbs unladen, throttled up and ready to go, they made the earth shake—way too heavy for the present landing strip. The plane was bought, however, and would be flown over from Canada when the runway was extended to receive it. But the survey had shown this henge, this long-kept secret of the field. Sir William had provided the disused farmhouse, and now we were engaged in a 'rescue dig—meant to salvage something of the deep past before it was destroyed.

Few if any of us kneeling over our Neolithic and Bronze Age site with our little cast trowels had been alive during the war; that was our parents' and grandparents' day. We were more concerned with time out of mind. We pored over the earth, seeking tiny clues about the prehistoric past. When we were done, the heavy bomber would be brought thundering in.

Little wonder, then, if we felt dislocated sometimes. Not dislocated, the place remained the same, the topography altered little. The range of hills, the plateau where we worked, the twin flowing rivers, the pines and cawing rooks—these were constant. But it was easy to feel unhooked from time, to be uncertain which era one was alive in. Under our knees, in the earth, a Neolithic henge, which was now beginning to yield Bronze Age artefacts too. In the air, the sound of the 'finest hour', the Hurricane lifting off from its grass strip. There was a lingering 1960s feel around the community of diggers—and, as I say, something of the seventeenth-century English radicals of that name, who were concerned to 'level all estates'. And now Margaret Thatcher, antithesis of all that, was chasing her new broom round Downing Street.

In his Battle of Britain speech, Churchill said this: 'If we open a quarrel between the past and the present, we shall find that we have lost the future.' There was no quarrel, because the past, the various pasts, were all present. It was what I'd felt in my fanciful visits to standing stones, that to level all estates, to abolish all layers of time, took only a little imagination.

On one of our long leisured evenings, a boyfriend and I slipped away from the farmhouse, away from the site altogether. We made our way down the steep defile to the meadow beside the Machany Water which was, and still is, just a tiny tree-lined burn. The burn was easy to cross, but the meadow on the far side felt like a faraway secluded place. There we discovered, parked in the buttercups and apparently forgotten, the fuselage of an aeroplane belonging to the aircraft museum. He said it was a DC10. I had never then been in an aeroplane, so, as no one was around, we scrambled up, slid into the cockpit and pretended to fly.

'Features' were the great excitement. Features happen when, under your trowel, a something, you know not what, a true earth mystery, begins to loom up. It might be just the surface of a stone, or a change in the colour of the earth: a hearth where a fire once burned stays black for ever. It's dusted with the hand, appraised. The archaeologist's skill is in telling a something from a nothing, human intentionality from nature or chance. They learn to read stones, but sometimes stones stay shtum. But it's a ruthless business: even as the mystery is revealed, it's dismantled and destroyed.

Each of the four assistant archaeologists wrote a daily logbook, in which they kept track of the progress of their portion of the site, and of 'features' as they emerged. The logbooks still exist: they are fawn-coloured A4 school jotters. 'Supplied for the Public Service', they say, which makes them historical artefacts in themselves. If something was unearthed that looked like it might develop into a feature, it was allocated a number. One can follow its progress day to day by checking that number in the logbooks. Many features come up, burst, vanish like bubbles in champagne.

Depending on which of the assistants is writing, the small regiment of volunteers, of whom I was one, is referred to variously as 'diggers', 'rabble' or even, sardonically, 'work units'. Which 'work unit' first happened upon Feature 455 I don't recall, and the logbook doesn't say. Lowly diggers were not entrusted with 'features'. If something exciting looked like it was emerging, backwards, like a dog out of hedge, a more experienced worker would be sent to take over. Of course, everyone knew when a feature was slowly being revealed. They were the subjects of our conversations, central to the life of the site.

Feature 455 became the responsibility of a pleasant man called John. There were several Johns, all with by-names. There was a John the Veg, who ate no meat, and raffish John the Pilot, to whom a certain glamour accrued because he did indeed hold a pilot's licence. This site, with its regular fly-pasts of WW2 planes, must have been a joy to him. But it was John the Tent who worked on 455. 'John's got himself a feature at last!' says the logbook. And later, 'John's feature worth all the fuss!'

The rest of us got on with our scraping and stripping down, but you could always find an excuse—dawdling back from emptying a wheelbarrow, for example—to wander over and see how other folk were doing. You could appraise someone else's little square of desert, or cast a glance into a post-hole. Everyone knew, therefore, that within the Neo-lithic enclosure other things were emerging, still prehis-toric, but of much more recent date. It meant that many centuries after the original celebrants were dead and gone, their enclosure was still potent, was still being used. In fact, it was used on and off for 2500 years. Whatever the henge had been, it lingered a long, long time in custom and memory.

Feature 455 began as the scratch of a stone under the edge of a trowel. A flattish stone, then next to it another, then a third and so on until an oval area, a sort of crazy paving, had emerged about five feet long and four wide. It was in an important place: well within the ancient enclosure but not at the exact centre.

Now there followed a process. Each newly revealed layer was cleaned of earth, drawn on paper plans, photographed and, in due course, removed, so the next layer down could be exposed, similarly mapped and then in turn removed and the next course of stones revealed. To add to the odd sensation of inhabiting several different times, there was also this process of dismantling; of running the narrative of construction backwards.

Thus, the arena of flattish stones was mapped, and removed. Under them were some more stabilising earth and stones, but the next layer down consisted in just one single, huge grey boulder. It was so big and heavy it must have taken several strong men to manoeuvre it into place. It had presence, and everyone now knew it was a capstone for a cist.

The Latinate 'inhumation' was a word I learned on that site; 'inhumation' being distinct from 'cremation' as a way of disposing of the dead, but the old word 'cist' I already knew. As 'kist' it lingers in Scots as the word for a chest or box; a corn chest or blanket chest is a kist. We quickly understood that John had unearthed a Bronze Age cist burial. Now the little covering pavement had been taken away, it was the huge rounded cover stone, or capstone, which had sealed the coffin for thousands of years, which was coming to light.

The weather remained unseasonably cold and windy. Being outdoors all day, we were attuned to that. When the long ridge of the Ochils was capped by grey clouds, the whole landscape became sullen and powerful. Between showers we worked on. Post-holes and ditches were fine, but now the site had focus. Here were 'earth mysteries' indeed; soon something would be uncovered which had lain in privacy and darkness for 3500 years.

For several days John worked to clean the capstone itself, and he was always ready to lean up from his task and give cheery progress reports. The archaeologists were excited by its state of preservation, no damage or collapse. John cleared an area around the capstone, so it lay exposed like a huge egg a step down from the surrounding ground. Then it was declared ready to be lifted; tomorrow would be the day.

I was darkly excited by the prospect. Many of us were—how could we fail to be? We were young and this cist burial was very, very old. Even the experienced hands were keen, and they were full of stories both ghoulish and tender. Had we heard about the labourer on a site in York who'd accidentally put his pickaxe through a sewage pipe? Not a sewage pipe: turned out to be a medieval lead coffin. *But what's that green sludge?* he'd asked. 'That's the body.' He'd fainted! Had we heard about the Bronze Age woman and her baby, buried together, laid on a swan's wing?

It was the last day of May. The fretful weather of the past week had steadied into a sullen gloom. In twos and threes we wandered out onto site at nine o'clock as usual, through the wooden gate and over the field toward the line of syca-mores and thence to the henge, scraped and bare. Within the ditch, within the sanctuary of the ring of post-holes, in its hollow was the waiting capstone. We set to our various tasks with trowels and drawing boards and measuring sticks. Low blue-dark cloud covered the whole sky, the hills were obscured.

————————

Though I remember that morning well, I've often wondered if I've elaborated it, and introduced a touch of Gothic fantasy, but recently a friend from those days, the boyfriend of the DC10, corroborated it. It was a very odd day.

There was more preparatory work to be done round the capstone, and that took an hour, until at mid-morning the call came to down tools and clear the site. By then the sky was even darker, more like November than May, but close and windless. A small yellow mobile crane, hired from a local firm, trundled onto site.

We 'diggers' herded ourselves onto the far side of the site and watched as the crane driver, called to an unusual task, conferred with the anxious archaeologists. Together they peered at the stone, crouched over it, stood in a huddle, discussed. There was a problem—a supporting stone beneath the capstone had shifted, allowing a spill of earth into the cist, threatening to destabilise the structure and spoil the contents, so, although the weather wasn't ideal, the task had become urgent. Against the spoil heaps and the black hills behind, the yellow, mechanical crane was a strange trump of modernity.

At last all was set—and this is the bit I recall. There was some final manoeuvring, and then the crane took possession of the capstone and began to lift it. At that moment, however, the instant we began to violate the grave, a tremendous clap of thunder rolled down from the hills. Even as the crane swung the capstone aside and laid it on the spoil heap, the hills announced their disapproval and, as we moved forward to see what the cist contained, more thunder came, and huge drops of rain began to fall, so immediately a tarpaulin was dragged over the grave, concealing it again from sight.

―――――

I fled the threat of the office job, the secretarial college, and spent the following winter in a cold dark cottage on the Orkney Islands, where I wrote a small poem, and called it 'Inhumation':

> No-one noticed if he opened his eyes,
> acknowledged the dark,
> felt around, found and drank
> the mead provided,
> supposing himself dead.

The opening of the cist had lingered in my mind. The whole summer had lingered in my mind, full of possibility. Of course it had—I was seventeen, just out of my big comprehensive school and my parents' semi. It was a turning place, a henge, a hinge indeed. The exams had been no triumph; if I'd thought about trying for university, which was not an easy process anyway, without a knowledgeable family or supportive teachers the idea was dashed anyway.

But you could sign on the dole. You could hide among the swelling numbers of genuinely unemployed, and claim a little money every week. That's what people did: artists, diggers, mountaineers, would-be poets and musicians, anarchists and feminists. Anyone for whom the threat of a job, of conformity, felt like death.

The opening of the cist under that thunderclap was thrilling, transgressive. So, in its quiet way, was writing poems. The weight and heft of a word, the play of sounds, the sense of carefully revealing something authentic, an artefact which didn't always display 'meaning', but which was a true expression of—what?—a self, a consciousness. This was thrilling too.

In the cist it wasn't a man, but a woman. Had I written 'she', 'supposing herself dead', my poem would have read like a metaphor, as a poem about myself. It wasn't about me. It was about the body in the cist.

———

She had been placed, as was the custom, on her right side, crouched with her legs drawn up, her head hard against the top wall of the cist. We looked down onto the skull and long leg bones, which were intact, and gleamed up from the bottom of the stone box, eerie and tender at once. But there was something uncomfortable about the turn and grin of the skull. The angle was wrong. Once the body was in place in the cist, someone had reached in and turned the dead girl's face to look upward, and toward the east. Then, beside her, they had placed that bowl with its grooved and jabbed decoration. It had been filled with mead flavoured with meadowsweet. Then they had laid the capstone over her.

It had done well, that food vessel. It had kept its long vigil. Because of the way it had toppled, perhaps the very moment the heavy capstone had been shifted into place, the skull and the bowl seemed to be gazing into each other, mouth to mouth, as though engaged in a long dialogue.

Rather than cooling the weather, the thunder seemed instead to herald the arrival of summer. June opened with clear blue skies and increasingly warm days. Work on site continued quickly—time was limited. Plan, draw, photograph, take it down. It was perfect flying weather; the vintage planes took off and landed. Dig and dismantle—there would be nothing left. Evidence suggests that many Neolithic sites and chambered cairns were not merely forgotten, but ritually closed. Rings of posts were burned in situ by those masters of fire, or stones heaped over the entrances to burial mounds. This work seemed an equivalent. A ritualised undoing.

Being no longer required, most of the 'diggers' left in the middle of June. There was a final party, of course, and because it was midsummer, it didn't really get dark. We stayed up all night and at dawn a few of us wandered down to the bigger river, the Earn, and sat under the arch of the old bridge. The water passing under the bridge in the dawn light was satiny, palest grey. Some bats flitted through the arches. I remember an earnest conversation, but what it was about I can't recall.

Some folks were going south, down to Stonehenge to mark the summer solstice, to see the sun rise over the Heel Stone and get into the mystic. There was always ribaldry about this, between the ley-line faction and those who scoffed. But the diggers, outdoors all day, with Neolithic dust under their fingernails, were closer to the spirit of the thing than any ridiculous berobed 'druids'.

I didn't go to Stonehenge, but instead left North Mains in the company of a long-haired lad called Pete the Joint and we hitched to the coast, all of thirty miles away, and slept on a headland. How vast the sea, after all that concentrating on a tiny patch of earth.

Others were moving on to different archaeological sites. It was a bit of a golden age; life as an itinerant 'digger' was not impossible, and not intolerable for a while, especially for the young, and we were all young. Every site was an information exchange. In that, the henge probably functioned as it had 4000 years ago. Whatever it was for, it was also a place for romances, graft, parties, huge pots of food and good-natured resentment of the bosses who seemed to know what they were doing. Our off-duty lives probably got us closer to the Neolithic or Bronze Age than any analysis of post-holes and bones.

————————

It would be simple to read much into the business of the Lancaster bomber rolling over the Neolithic henge, the Bronze Age cemetery, but I think it would be trite. It was nothing more than a bizarrerie. Besides, the 'readings' wouldn't tell us anything we don't already know. We know we are a species obsessed with itself and its own past and origins. We know we are capable of removing from the sanctuary of the earth shards and fragments, and gently placing them in museums. Great museums in great cities—the hallmarks of civilisation.

We are also capable of fire-bombing those cities, and melting their citizens to what Kurt Vonnegut called a 'foul stew'. Vonnegut was a POW in Dresden, detailed to remove the bodies after the US bombers and Lancasters had done their worst. Flight had certainly revealed something of the face of the earth, and also the face of our own capacities. We can reach into a cist-grave and turn the face of the dead girl toward the light, and place a bowl of sweet food in with her, to tide her over into the beyond. At Dresden, the people had crammed themselves into cellars, into cists, hoping to be safe. It was impossible to remove the bodies for burial. They sent in a man with a flame-thrower.

I didn't know it thirty years ago, but Neolithic sites were often built at the confluence of two rivers, so when I crossed the bridge on the way back to North Mains it was with a different awareness. Prehistoric people would have made the crossing by coracle, or something, and the crossing would have been of ritual significance, an arrival at the centre of the world, a plateau site held in place by the surrounding hills.

It was May again, the track was the same, rooks cawed, and the farmhouse, far from being demolished, had new windows and a well-to-do lived-in look. When a light aircraft took off and began circling round overhead, I nearly laughed. What's thirty years in the scheme of things? It wasn't a Hurricane, though, but a bright blue Cessna. A

field away beyond the farmhouse stood the same row of sycamores, with fresh leaves. Beyond the sycamores, where the
henge had been, there was no sign of a runway at all.

No one answered the doorbell, so I made my way to the
sycamores, then stood beneath them, trying to recall where
exactly in the expanse of fallow field the henge had been.

The henge was gone, of course, we saw to that. But the
runway had never been built. Or, if it had, it had been
grubbed up again pretty soon. The Lancaster had arrived
alright, but a few short years after the excavation the aircraft
museum closed, and the entire collection was sold off. The
Lancaster was flown south, but a hangar roof collapsed on it,
and what was left was broken up for spares.

The henge is gone, the director's report is available to
read, the photos are filed away, the Bronze Age woman's
bones—well, they're in a cardboard box in a city store. The
food vessel is reunited with its sister, and displayed in the
National Museum, and has nothing to do with this place,
this here.

This here. This same topography. I walked out into the
middle of the fallow field on its plateau. With the enclosing
hills and twin, east-flowing rivers, it is still the landscape
the Neolithic people had understood so acutely, the same
earth into which the Bronze Age woman had been lowered.
Eastward, vanishing into haze, lay the river valley I'd driven
that morning, where once the wild aurochs roamed.

You are placed in landscape, you are placed in time. But,
within that, there's a bit of room for manoeuvre. To some
extent, you can be author of your own fate. At least, that's
what I'd been lucky enough to learn.

THE GANNETRY

———

the whole pageantry

of the year was
awake tingling
near

the edge of the sea

—W. CARLOS WILLIAMS

THE COLONY WAS OBVIOUS: half a mile ahead, a column of birds turned bright and white in the summer air. They were visible as a loose plume as we walked over the island toward them, and doubtless visible for miles out to sea. It was exciting, like a fun fair; the closer we got to the cliff edge the more we could hear the racket, the more the breeze brought us the smell.

The cliffs were south-facing, full in the sun, and five hundred foot high. They formed promontories and bowls, so we walked out onto the broadest promontory and from there looked back into the cauldron the birds had commandeered for themselves. All was squalor and noise: the birds' tenement was so plastered with guano that it shone, and the airborne birds cast winged shadows on the whitewashed walls. Under these soothing shadows thousands more gannets were installed all along the cliff's ledges, tier above tier. The flying birds were perfectly silent. Those on the cliff, though, made a loud fretful noise. They were caught up in constant greetings, and constant disputes: about each other, about thefts and incursions, about the indignity of it all—the one demand the empty future makes of them: breed! breed!

Tim and I grinned at each other. This was what we wanted: a full-blown seabird colony at the height of June.

Earlier on we'd crossed an imaginary line marked by a little roadside sign which said '60'. Not a speed limit—it announced the degree of latitude. Tonight there would be no dark, only an hour or two of 'simmer dim' as the Shetland people say—a twilit stillness at midnight, as though the sun were holding its breath. Now, though, it was mid-afternoon, and the hottest day of the year so far. The sun was high, spilling over the sea, lighting the cliff, and every stone and every bird. And every flower. All around us on the sloping clifftop, tufts of pink thrift were in bloom. Each flowerhead shivered in the breeze.

When I was small, thick brass threepenny bits were still in circulation. A few had an image of thrift, three flowers of course, being three (old) pence on the 'tails' side. I remember my father explaining the clever little pun that moved between the coin's modest amount and the flower called thrift. I was enchanted by it. But what spread before us here was abundance and profligacy—the wide sea under a high white-clouded sky, the cascading light, the public clamour of thousands of seabirds. Sometimes we caught the wistful smell of the flowers, but mostly it was ammonia and bird shit, carried up on the breeze. Bird shit and pink thrift, the smell of summer.

On a flat stone the size of a door, near but not too near the edge, Tim and I sat down and began to watch in silence, each entering a private, visual world, sometimes using binoculars, sometimes not. In the water far below were rocks and small stacks, with surf breaking around them.

Just off the cliff edge, a few yards away from where we sat, gannet after gannet beat by, with outstretched beaks and hard eyes, taking the corner into the colony at speed, as if bearing urgent dispatches. We were close enough to see their eyes, and they are sharp-sighted, but if they noticed us they made no sign. We were nothing, land things, and gannets disdain land. They disdain land, but every spring they're lured to their traditional cliffs and stacks by a siren song. Never a summer that isn't spent like this, in fuss and bother, each pair raising a single chick.

After a few minutes, I said: 'It seems like a long time ago.'

'What does?'

I gestured to the bird-crowded cliff face. I meant the time of breaking waters and nappy buckets and trails of milky vomit down one's shoulder. 'Over!' I laughed. 'That bit's over. For me, anyway.'

———————

Tim and I have been friends for years, since our respective children were babies. He works as a radio producer for the

BBC. In fact, we met when he asked me to write what he called a 'radio poem' for broadcast and I wanted to very much. I was anxious to feel I was still in the game, could still think, because with a new, hungry baby my mind had melted into a puddle of feeds and laundry, and my real life seemed to have been mislaid.

Now we skive off once a year or so to see some birds. This was today's plan. We'd been lucky with the weather, so now we'd surrender ourselves to the uproar of breeding gannets. For me, not an ornithologist, the colony was sheer sound and spectacle. A thousand vignettes unfolded on the screen, the cliff face in front of me. Arrivals and departures, bondings and squabbles and fights. Some birds were greeting each other with long upraised necks, others hung in the air, bodies and necks suspended below their wings as though the wings were held up by invisible pegs. We'd watch gannets, and whatever else happened by. There were puffins and Arctic skuas, too. Tim's a good birder, and he likes the unexpected. If some rarity turned up, he'd see it, and he'd say.

———

To service the colony required a constant airlift, a bringing in of relief and supplies. Every minute, birds were turning our corner into the colony. They are not small, and they're not tentative. Each commanded its space, whether in the air or on the ledges where they made their fuss.

Urr-urr, they said, from way down in the throat. As some arrived, others were departing at speed, silent, heading straight out to sea. I tried to watch individuals, to follow particular narratives, but to no avail; each story wove into another. Here they were in the air, gannet, gannet, repeated like a stammer, the whole idea of gannet amplified and displayed. On the cliff, each pair had its own precise space, just out of reach of the next, and these spaces were well policed. Whenever a bird landed, with its big wings flapping, all the neighbours raised a hue and cry, and that set off a chain reaction; so all over the cliff there were outbreaks of noise and aggression; more harsh urr-urr and wings and long stabbing beaks.

But, under the bother, many birds were sitting incubating. I presume they were incubating, that they had eggs under their bellies, under their black webbed feet. Once folded and settled, they seemed able to enter a dwam, as Scots say. They could shut out all the noise, and face inward, to gaze at the cliff face inches in front of them. When gannets close their wings, the tips form a cross at the back. All over the white-stained cliff, I could see nests made of seaweed, and that each nest was marked with a black cross.

'D'you remember that one with the rope?' I called to Tim. He was looking out to sea through binoculars, elbows resting on drawn-up knees, concentrating. He nodded, he could hardly have forgotten. It had been a couple of years before and we'd been on a boat and seen a gannet flying overhead, with six or eight feet of rope dangling from its gullet; discarded rope it must have mistaken for a fish, and plunged for, and tried to swallow. I can picture it still, silhouetted against the sky, its cruciform shape and this rope unspooled from its beak, unnerving and apocalyptic.

'So much plastic tat here, too. Look at it all!'

Their nests are just padded-down rings of seaweed, each bird sat on top of seaweed on top of a trail of white droppings, but woven into the nests were shreds of nylon rope, orange and blue, or scraps of net. In one was a length of that flat stuff used to bind parcels, the kind that whips back if you cut it with a Stanley knife. It was a blue line against the white cliff and it caught my eye because one end was playing in the breeze. But a neighbouring bird had spied it, too, and reached out along the ledge with a surreptitious beak, and gently, carefully, began to steal it away. Creatures of the eye, they see what they want and want what they see, just like the rest of us.

Just then, a commotion broke out, even more of a stramash than usual. About halfway down the cliff two birds were fighting, seriously this time. Their big beaks were scissored together and, as they tussled, both beat with heavy wings, striving to stay on the ledge. But one of them fell off and began to tumble down the cliff, passing level below level of identical birds. There was nothing else to do but watch it fall in disarray toward the sea, but as I did so an image came to mind. It was a painting, 'Landscape with the Fall of Icarus' by Breughel. In that picture, Icarus, strapped to his white feathery wings, has already plunged into the green water. He's drowning. Only his little legs stick up. No one has noticed: not the ship sailing by, not the distant white city, especially not the peasant in the foreground, ploughing his field. What, the painting asks, is the fate of one boy—or one bird—in the scheme of things? Then, though, the gannet opened his wings, was lifted by the air, and lost in the multitude.

I lowered the glasses again. This was exhausting. Exhilarating, but exhausting. What it must be for them, this breeding business. Shredded nerve and argy-bargy and sexual tension, and the young weren't even hatched yet. The birds' noise purled on up into the warm afternoon air. They held their long beaks at every angle, like—paintings again—those portraits of aristocratic dynastic families, where everyone is elegant and looks into the distance, looks anywhere except at each other. Thus it would all continue till the season was over, and it was a long season. It could be September before the young were fledged and the adults quit for their other lives, the silent scrutiny of the sea.

'D'you suppose there are any who just don't bother? Any gannets who fly in and take one look at all this, and think yuk, and head straight back out to sea?'

'My dear, the noise, the people.' Shouldn't think so.

'I suppose they're at the mercy of their own instincts. No option.'

'Actually, they're doing a lot of research into homosexuality in seabirds.'

We watched quietly for a while more, just with the sound of the birds and the surf. Then Tim called, 'Pomarine skua! Beyond the rocks . . . heading left, dark, low over the waves . . . did you get it? Did you see its spoons?'

He meant its tail feathers, which twist into a spoon shape. I saw the bird, briefly, but I didn't see its spoons. If ever I had that acuity of vision, I don't now.

It was mid-afternoon. Wind and sun in our faces. To the west, the headlands of the Shetland mainland receded away southward. If you sailed, or flew—strapped to your dubious wings—due east, you'd be heading for Bergen. The sun was still high. We'd brought a bit of a picnic, so unpacked that and, using our rock as a table, ate cheese and oatcakes and apples. Sometimes a big wave sent a booming echo up from below. Thrift bloomed between rocks, the birds came and went, the noise and smell, like a smog, curled up from the colony. Gannets can fly far in search of food; that's why their numbers are holding up well. It's the puffins and guillemots and kittiwakes that are struggling to feed their young in a depleted sea.

It had been a while since I'd thought about those baby days—the intense early weeks. And to be reminded of it by gannets, of all things. I'd always quite fancied the gannet life. Seen from the shore or out on a boat, it looked like the radical alternative. All air and light and ocean waves, rigorous and austere. Whether glinting against a storm cloud, or folding themselves into a dagger, to plunge for fish, gannets seemed more mind than body, more mineral than animal. I like to watch lone gannets interrogating the sea, like some old patrician poet frowning over his papers. And here they were, en masse. It was quite funny, really, to hear them make this flagrant din. Yes, even gannets: highly strung, noisy, aggravated and frustrated after all, crammed together in a domestic order that looked like chaos.

When we'd eaten enough, I wiped my hands on my jacket and picked up the binoculars again, but this time turned away from the cliff with all its squalor and dramas, and looked instead down at the sea below. There were yet more gannets down there. A club of juveniles occupied a flat terrace of rock at the cliff-foot, twenty or so birds in mottled plumage who had come back from their early wanderings, summonsed by that breeding instinct. Not yet old enough to do it, but old enough to take an interest. Out on the water, before the waves broke, were more adults, a raft of them riding up and down on the slight swell. The binoculars framed three or four at a time. Each white breast caught the sunshine, and against that white the water appeared an impenetrable dark blue.

There was no particular reason to look there, except that it was restful. The birds maybe found it restful, too, compared to the colony. Perhaps they were just stealing a little time before heading back into the fray.

The gannets rode the water a couple of hundred yards out, and I looked down at them from the clifftop, without thinking much. Actually, I was beginning to wonder about the time. We'd have to make a move soon, to get the last little boat off the island at the end of the day. The day according to the clock, that is. The sun would be high for hours yet. Small waves rolled in, and on the waves the gannets lifted and fell.

Just then, though, I began to realise that there was something in my field of vision that hadn't been there before. It was as though someone had leaned over my shoulder and drawn, among the resting birds, a quick vertical line with a pencil. That's all. A quick line. I thought it was perhaps a mirage, a trick of the light—it was a bit wavery. Or just a creel marker that had lost its flag. But it didn't bob like a creel marker.

It was probably nothing, so I said nothing, but kept looking. That's what the keen-eyed naturalists say. Keep looking. Keep looking, even when there's nothing much to see. That way your eye learns what's common, so when the uncommon appears, your eye will tell you.

My eye told me that there were gannets, riding on the waves and, among them, an oddity, a vertical pencil line. This seeing, wordless and intent, lasted only a few seconds, but felt longer. Sealed off from the gannets' noise and the surf and the sky, held in a tunnel of my own vision that linked the clifftop to the sea, hundreds of feet below, I was curious now, and concentrating. I could feel the moments unfold. It was surely growing taller, this dark line. It was acquiring presence. Then two of the nearby birds began to flap their wings, ready to take off. They'd been disturbed. Something was happening underneath them, under the water's surface. The birds lumbered into the air, and at that moment the black line turned into profile, and I realised what it was.

The baby days are over. My son is old enough to have his own mobile phone, and to be droll. Later I sent him a text, 'Saw 5 killer whales!', and he came back, 'Not bad for a day's work!' He can look me level in the eye now, and laugh and say: 'In three years I'll be able to get married! Drive a car!' 'Fine,' I reply. 'But first can you pick your dirty underpants up off the floor?'

Tim was onto the killer whales as soon as I hollered, as soon as I leaned over and thumped him, delighted, yelling about fins. Three fins were clear of the water now, jet-black and sheeny, the male's on the outside so tall, as tall as a man, that the sun dazzled off it. With a slow sea motion they rolled up, fin first, then backs so broad the seawater spilled off on either side, then we saw their nearsides, a medley of white and black. As those three tilted back down in unison, Tim swung to sit beside me, calling, 'Two more, just behind!' And indeed, two more fins, shorter and more hooked than the male's, were appearing up through the water's surface. There was something about that second pair, a collusion or privacy, which made me wonder if they were mother and young. Then they in turn blew, and began to roll under the surface, and the water closed over them as if they'd never been.

For a few moments there was only sea, and gannets passing below us, with outstretched necks. Then, farther along rightwards, and side by side, the first three fins began to rise again, appearing from underwater into the visible world of light and birds.

Tim said a party of gannets appeared to be following the animals, as gulls follow the plough, and it was so, but the gannets, lately so impressive, suddenly seemed flappy, airy little things, next to the orca's greater presence. And exposed: the killer whales revealed only as much of themselves as was necessary; much more of their bodies remained concealed from us under the sea's surface, even when they blew, but the birds were all there, all visible.

The procession was travelling eastward, following the curve of the island, and because that was the direction we'd have to take to reach the jetty Tim and I packed up hastily, left the gannets to their ruckus and began to run over the turf. We jumped rocks and tufts of pink thrift, avoided rabbit holes, and ran along trying to keep up, trying to keep the animals in view down in the water at our left, calling, 'There!' when they rolled up to breathe. When they appeared they were a stern, tight black and white, visible for a long moment against the wide loose blues of the sea and sky, and then they slowly rolled down and then gone. I stopped to catch my breath and look away out to the horizon. All this was happening in a tiny corner of the sea, but the sea suddenly seemed different. It appeared vaster, more alive and knowing and expressive than before.

We hurried a mile downhill, down to sea level, until we stood breathless and jubilant on a rocky shore, looking out over the water, but the animals had entered a broad band of glare far too bright for our human eyes, and that was that.

————

Gannets glitter. They're made for vision, shine in any available light, available to see and be seen. Their eyes are round and fierce, with a rim of weird blue, and they are adapted to see down through the surface reflections of the sea. There, they take what they need—and what they don't. Less patrician poet, more bargain-hunter. 'A butter-scoop, a battledoor, a golf-ball, some toy whips, some little baskets and a net-maker's needle' are just some of the oddities found in gannets' nests,—but that quaint list was compiled a century ago, when an ornithologist called J. H. Gurney published an earnest, learned book called simply *The Gannet*. All that was then known of the bird's history and natural history is there. A battledoor is a sort of tennis racket, and what would a gannet want with one of those? But the acquisitive habit continues, hence the shredded polyprop rope and nylon net. Sometimes the youngsters get entangled in this stuff, and die like that, hanged from their natal cliffs before they can fly.

I read later that orca live in family groups, and that what I'd assumed, with slight world-weariness, was a dominant male with one or two adult females, 'his' females and his offspring, was nothing of the kind. They are matriarchal; a son remains with his mother. In a year or so, god willing, my son will indeed be taller than I am. When he measures himself against me, and gloats, I'll poke him in the chest and say, 'Just be glad you're not a killer whale, pal.'

We learned, too, that this was a resident group, following a regular beat around the islands; they were not a rare occurrence. But I remember how that huge fin manifested itself in front of my eyes, a private miracle. For days after I felt different, looser of limb, thrilled because the world had thrown me a gift and said, 'Catch!'

The real rarity, apparently, was Tim's Pomarine skua, with its spoons, which was the first ever recorded for Noss.

Sometimes in winter, when the dark comes early and presses at the window, and I'm feeling landlocked, I think about gannets. Or gannetries, rather. There are gannet stations all around the coast; some have been active for centuries. Grassholm, Little Skellig, Ailsa Craig: I can rhyme off their names. Stac Lee and Stac an Armin on St Kilda, Sula Sgeir and Sule Stack out in the Atlantic and named after 'solan', which is the gannet. Hermaness, at the very north of Shetland, Noss, Troup Head, The Bass, Bempton: stacks and sea-cliffs and flat-topped rocks. Actually, The Bass Rock is far from remote: it's near as dammit in the city, you can see it from the windows of the John Lewis store in Edinburgh, a shining beacon of bird shit in the Firth of Forth. You can imagine gannetries like you imagine lighthouses. Romantic outposts, if you please, facing down the wild sea—but without all that rugged manliness. They're wild and far-flung, but domestic, ignoble, noisy, seasonal.

My son grows tall, my daughter lives in a girls' web of thrills and tensions invisible to me. She frets about who said what to whom, and who sent what text; sometimes whole days are spent in fallings out and makings up and social anxiety. I want to say it doesn't matter. 'It does matter!' says my daughter, and she's right.

What is the fate of one gannet? If a chick is hatched too late in the season, its parents may simply abandon it on its ledge, when instinct calls them back out to sea: 'Everything turns away / quite leisurely from the disaster.' Back to sea until the spring comes, and the thrift blooms, bringing again its one imperative—breed!

––––––––––

What might just save us, according to the naturalist Edward O. Wilson, is a quirk. More than a quirk, 'An almost miraculous gift of human nature to future generations' which we're only just noticing. By human nature, Wilson means women's nature. We don't 'breed'. When women have the choice, and health and a measure of prosperity, we immediately risk having fewer children, or none. Wilson calls it an instinct: 'A universal instinctive choice'. He says that it might just happen that, over the next century, through women's empowerment and health care for infants, human numbers will stabilise then begin to fall. In turn, human demands on the planet will reduce, too, and we might avert a catastrophe, and carry ourselves, and innumerable other species, into the times to come. It's a good vision. A kind of thrift. Raise one or two children, who, disaster aside, will become healthy adults, then you're free go back to watching the sea.

Sometimes I think about the killer whales, too, another kind of vision—the sudden unexpected. They were unmistakable, black and white, showing us only as much of themselves as they had to. If ever I see a pod of killer whales again, I'll regard that male, six-foot, filmstar fin differently. I'll wonder which of the others is the matriarch.

So we go on. Next summer the gannets will be back from the sea to their colonies, going through the whole palaver again. Sometimes they fly alone, and sometimes one behind the other in long fast ribbons just above the waves, with urgency in their beating wings and outstretched necks.

LIGHT

—

EVERY YEAR, IN THE THIRD WEEK OF FEBRUARY, there is a day, or, more usually, a run of days, when one can say for sure that the light is back. Some juncture has been reached, and the light spills into the world from a sun suddenly higher in the sky. Today, a Sunday, is such a day, though the trees are still stark and without leaves; the grasses are dry and winter-beaten.

The sun is still low in the sky, even at noon, hanging over the hills southwest. Its light spills out of the southwest, the same direction as the wind: both sunlight and wind arrive together out of the same airt, an invasion of light and air out of a sky of quickly moving clouds, working together as a swift team. The wind lifts the grasses and moves the thin branches of the leafless trees and the sun shines on them, in one movement, so light and air are as one, two aspects of the same entity. The light is razor-like, edging grasses and twigs of the willow and apple trees and birch. The garden is all left-leaning filaments of light, such as you see on cobwebs, mostly, too hard to be called a sparkle, too metallic, but the whole garden's being given a brisk spring-clean. Where there are leaves, such as the holly 200 yards away, the wind lifts the leaves and the sun sweeps underneath. All moving because of the fresh wind.

Now the town's jackdaws are all up in a crowd, revelling in the wind, chack-chacking at each other. And I hear a girl's voice, one of my daughter's friends, one of the four girls playing in the garden. She makes a call poised just between play and fear. What are they playing? Hide and seek? No matter. It pleases me that my daughter says they are 'playing in the garden', because they're eleven years old; another year or two and they wouldn't admit to 'playing' at all, and for a while the garden will have no appeal, because everything they want will be elsewhere. For a few years they'll enter a dark mirror-tunnel whose sides reflect only themselves.

The girls themselves can't be seen, obscured by trees and that edgy, breezy light. The year has turned. Filaments and metallic ribbons of wind-blown light, just for an hour, but enough.

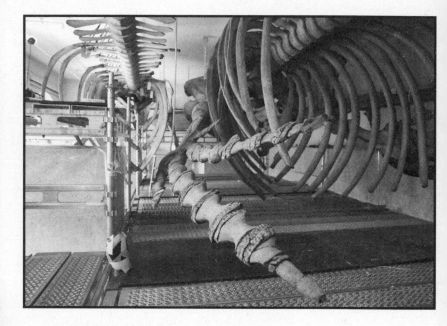

THE HVALSALEN

BECAUSE OF ITS HILLTOP POSITION, up by the university, the Bergen Natural History Museum overlooks much of the old town. Conversely, it can be seen, with its grand arched windows, from almost everywhere. Steep streets run down directly to the harbours and fish market. It's a mid-nineteenth-century classical historicist building, set in semi-formal gardens. The façade is painted pale greyish-yellow, with grey mullions round the windows. It hasn't changed much, outside or in, since it opened in 1865.

One dull day in March, when Bergen was in thaw and great mounds of gritty snow lay at street corners, I pushed open the intimidating front door, made my way upstairs. The walls of the stairway bristled with the skulls and antlers of deer mounted on boards and, like a kind of doorman, a human skeleton hung in a glass case, but he didn't ask for my ticket. I wandered through the obligatory displays of stuffed birds, that mainstay of nineteenth-century museums:

a snowy owl eternally offering prey to its fluffy chicks; dull-eyed, long-dead ravens.

Then came the most prestigious room, the main hall. And there, entering through its double-height, double doors, I was taken aback. The architect must have intended a grand room—big enough to host a sizeable dance, or a city congregation—with thick wooden floors and cream-coloured pillars rising toward elaborate capitols, and arches, and arched windows, but the symmetry he intended was confounded because of the whales. The skeletons of the whales. You walk through into the 'Hvalsalen' and, immediately above, side by side, like vast oxen yoked together to haul the most terrible plough, are the jaws of two great baleen whales. Not just the jaws—the entire skeletons, the ribcages, the great fans of the scapulas and fin-bones, at the sides, the long receding trains of the spines. The bones are brown with age—and there are not one or two but twenty-four cetacean skeletons crowded under the ceiling. Four and twenty! Whales like sardines! Some faced east, some faced west. And dolphins, too, and, on the floor, raised on something like bed-legs, was a stuffed basking shark, with its terrible gills, and in a corner the skull of a sperm whale—dense, complex convolutions of bone.

The Hvalsalen. Whale Hall. What else could it be called? They were all there, such a roster of whales—the baleen whales—sei and humpback, right, fin and minke whales—even the blue whale, and the toothed whales too, sperm and bottlenose, narwhal and beluga, and the beaked Sowerby's whale, and, affixed to the walls, dolphins, almost dainty in comparison; the killer whale and the bottlenose.

Such bones as I never saw, hanging above my head.

There were glass cases, too, with sea creatures, sponges, crabs, starfish, but I barely glanced at those, being too enthralled with the skeletons overhead, their stoic majesty.

Of course, the blue whale was largest of all. I decided to walk under its full length, and count my steps. First, I walked under the smooth horizontal arch of the jaw, and its palate, where the baleen had once hung, sheets of age-browned bone. Then came the solid complications of the skull, now under the barrel of the ribcage, the ribs curving down, enclosing and protecting nothing but air. I kept walking, counting. As I passed the basking shark I surreptitiously touched its cold skin, rough as sandpaper. I passed a dolphin, small and lithe, and making for the door. Still the blue whale went on overhead. Above the basking shark hung a huge sunfish, an eerie-looking object hanging from a wire, more like a black moon with an eye. Still I walked on, counting until the spine ended. Fifty-seven paces. Less an animal, more a narrative. The ancient mariner.

On a central pillar, neatly painted in Norwegian and English were the words 'Do not touch the animals', but it was a bit late for that. The whalers' harpoons had got them, the flensing iron. Where else could the whales have come from? All, presumably, had met their deaths through violence, in the days of industrial whaling. A combination of nineteenth-century whaling and collecting—someone surely must have sent out commissions to whaling captains—bring me a blue! A beluga! A sperm whale's head on a plate! There was even a right whale—right for all the wrong reasons, hanging in its own space, cramped against the windows, up where the windows arched.

In the way of old-fashioned museums, there was next to nothing in the way of explanations or information aside from some handpainted signs dangling from the skeletons: 'Finnhval 1867. 15.7m.', 'Blahval. 24m. Finnmark 1879'.

But despite the weight of bones, the effect of the Hvalsalen was dreamlike. The vast structures didn't seem to offer any reproach. Rather, they drew you in. Undisturbed for a century, they had colluded to create a place of silence and memory. A vast statement of fact: 'Whales is what we were. This is what we are. Spend a little time here and you too feel how it is to be a huge mammal of the seas, to require the sea to hold you, to grow so big at the ocean's hospitality.'

Quite whale-freighted, I sat on a deep window ledge. Behind, through the little panes, were views of the town, under a cold mist. Above hung the right whale. No one else had entered the hall, I had been quite alone. But then came the high voices of schoolchildren, and quick footsteps. I thought, Now the atmosphere will break, but the kids and their teachers were en route elsewhere; they passed right by, a quick bright shoal darting through the Hvalsalen.

I left the museum by its great wooden front door, and crossed the cobbled forecourt. What a strange place that had been. The *presence* of all those whales' bones—they'd got under my skin, so to speak, so much so I stood there in the cold unsure what to do, where to go next.

For some reason I glanced back at the building. On its first floor, behind the three central arched windows, was

a spectral figure—a long white skeletal hand, lengthways against the window-glass, visible to all the town. It was the pectoral fin of the right whale.

I thought, To hang with it, turned and went back in.

Maybe too few people are sufficiently keen on whalebones to want to talk about them, because two curators were kind enough to interrupt their day to meet me. Or perhaps they feared they'd be dealing with someone upset or outraged by it all. Either way, I was greeted by a younger man, fit and strong, as so many young Norwegians appear to be, called

Terje Lislevand, who was an ornithologist. He accompanied a more senior figure, a petite dark woman called Anne Karin Hufthammer, who was the head of osteology herself. It was her Whale Hall, so to speak. More osteology than you could shake a stick at.

They led me back upstairs to the Whale Hall, and for half an hour or so I enjoyed a private guided tour. We spoke about whales, and whale relics. They reckoned Bergen's was probably the world's largest collection of whale specimens, but it was little known. In fact, the whole museum had been built on whales. That is to say, whale specimens had been exchanged or bartered from here all over the world. They had been sent, for example, to Switzerland. I neglected to ask what Switzerland had offered in return, or whether the landlocked Swiss, when presented with a whale's rib, would know what they were looking at. Perhaps, like Odysseus's oar, they'd mistake it for a flail.

They showed me a rare 'right-handed' narwhal, with the tusk growing from its right tooth, rather than the left. They pointed out the great whales' pelvic bones, which were small and delicate, like paper boats, and which hung under the immense spines. Dr Hufthammer said these were of special interest to evolutionary biologists and specimens were rare. These were all that remained of the whales' sojourn on land, millions of years ago, early in their evolutionary history. When the whales, or proto-whales, took to the seas, they lost their legs and their pelvises shrank away to this.

Then Dr Hufthammer stopped by a glass case, asking, 'Have you seen this?' Within the case was a spherical object, two feet across, dense and mean, like a huge swollen black eye. It was the heart of a killer whale. A deep red and black biological engine, with a sprig of aorta reaching out of it.

'It's not a model?'

'No, it is real, but we don't know how it is preserved. We daren't open it to find out, because of the chemicals.'

I wanted to tell her I'd seen killer whales, moving at speed in the surf round a Scottish island, so I could imagine that immense heart pounding in action. I wanted to tell about the human shapes and forms I'd become acquainted with in the medical museums in Edinburgh, little rag-tags and bob-tails fixed in their glass jars all with their own meanings, but nothing on this scale.

If the issue of whaling was at all sensitive, I didn't know. The Norwegians still hunt minke whales, you could buy whale-meat at the fish market down the hill, but it couldn't be avoided. I broached it by saying, 'I presume these whales were all hunted . . . ?'

'Actually, the Hvalsalen is a bit of a mystery. There is no record of how they got here . . . or how they got inside the building . . . how they were prepared.'

We were moving back toward the door, under the jaws of the humpback, when Terje said, 'You know the museum is closing . . . ?'

'No! I'd no idea . . . Closing for ever?'

'For four years. It's being closed for renovation and repair. The building, the exhibits, everything. We are all moving out!'

After 130 years, the offices and laboratories were packing up and moving to different quarters, to make room for new exhibition space. A bright, modernised Natural History Museum would reopen to the public in due course.

I'd been lucky to turn up when I had. At the risk of being rude I said, 'You know, I hope this Whale Hall won't change. It has such . . . *atmosphere.*'

A metaphysical atmosphere, if you like, where you could ponder human attitude to other creatures, their pain and our rapaciousness, and the strange beauty of their forms. That's what I felt, anyway, but I didn't want to announce that to two stern-minded Norwegian scientists I'd only just met, and who were, after all, in charge of the place.

However, they began speaking together and, though it was in Norwegian, I got the impression that the future of the Hvalsalen had been the subject of some debate. Then they laughed, and Anne turned back to me with a smile of satisfaction. It had indeed been discussed, and she had pre-vailed. She had overcome 'the minimalisers', as she called them. The Hvalsalen would not be changed.

'Good.'

'It will be a new, old exhibition!'

However, she went on, there was unavoidable work to be done.

'They are all are very dirty. Perhaps dangerous—maybe they will fall! Look—'

She led me to the arched windows, and pointed up to the right whale, the one I'd seen from the street, the one who'd made me come back in again. The poor right whales: they had taken the worst of it. Now, under her direction, I could see cracks in the ribs, fractures, bits fallen off . . .

'There is much damage. Also, you see up here . . .'

Now Anne pointed up to the last few tapering yards of the fin whale's spine. The vertebrae deepened in colour as they reduced in size, until the last were treacle-brown and sticky-looking.

'And here, too, on this one—this brown colour? It's oil. The oil is still coming, the dirt sticks to the oil . . .'

'*Still?*'

Poor whales, didn't they know when to stop? The same whale oil that greased the machines and lit the streets and parlours, the oil of soap and margarine. All that oil! Here they were, dead for a century, still giving out oil.

So that's how it was. Very soon, the Hvalsalen's doors would close to the public. An international team of specialist conservationists had been hired and would shortly arrive, and for two years they'd work on the great whales. All the grime and oil and dust of a long century would be carefully cleaned away. They'd make sure the skeletons had been hung correctly, anatomically speaking. They would take the chance to learn what more they could about the collection. Everything would be examined: the bones themselves, but also the chains and fixings that bore the tremendous weight, so there would be no danger of a whale jaw crashing down on someone's head.

'Will you lower them down?'

'No. It's not possible. They would collapse.'

Instead the conservation team would build scaffold and platforms, and spend their working days up amongst the whales themselves.

'What an extraordinary project—the cleansing of the whales!'

Terje said that if I wished to return later in the year, when the conservation team was here and it was all under way, that would be fine. In fact, they'd probably be glad of a visitor.

———

Five months later, in the closing days of August, when a hint of autumn was already in the Bergen air, I climbed through a hatch, crept out onto a plywood floor, and found myself standing high in the Hvalsalen windows, next to the freshly cleaned right whale. It was astonishingly light—it seemed to radiate such a thick yellow light. The word that came to mind was 'buttery'. The bones, I mean.

Beside me, project director Gordon Turner Walker stood with his arms folded, as though awaiting a verdict.

Buttery. The whole whale, suspended from its chains, there in front of us, all the smoothed and honed bones, seemed to emit a yellowish light.

'It's so bright!' I said.

'It's bleached underneath—I think that's been light reflected off snow that's done that. But yes, two kilogrammes of dust came off it. That's how sad we are—we weighed the dust! Conservation, though—once you've established the protocol, it's just glorified housework.'

I went nearer. A silence, an aura, call it what you will, emanated from the skeleton too, as though the bones recalled their flesh. You could kneel and look into the ribcage, like a huge sprung barrel; you could accompany the spine as it journeyed shoulder height across the room, broad as the toppled trunk of an old tree, vertebra after vertebra. Between each vertebra were cork spacers where in life there had been cartilage.

'These are fantastic shapes . . .' I said, stroking the spinous process, '. . . like plumes on helmets—it's like a single file of Romans marching by.'

'Don't!' said Gordon, laughingly. 'Don't get me started! I love bone.'

I looked a little longer—and began to realise there was a smell, too, when you got close. Warm and slight, not unpleasant, it seemed to be seeping from within the bones, as though cleaning them had released it from a long imprisonment. It was the smell of something from,—oh—a long time ago, early days at primary school.

The vertebrae in front of me felt grainy, not quite cold, and very slightly waxy.

'Wax crayons! That's the smell! The thick ones—"chubby stumps", we called them.'

'Probably made of whale oil,' Gordon said. 'Most things were.'

We paused.

He said, 'You know why they were called right whales, don't you?'

I nodded. The skeleton seemed to emit a nineteenth-century glow. You could imagine the kind of light a whale-oil lamp would have cast, on the corner of some Victorian street.

'Yup,' he said. 'A million whales up in smoke, and this is all we've got to show for it.'

Gordon was a Yorkshireman who had spent years in Norway, a specialist conservator with, he'd soon told me, a love of bone. That was his speciality. Archaeological bone. 'Bone is my passion, a beautiful material, a wonderful material . . .'

We were much the same age, late forties, and he was dressed all in black, black jeans, black T-shirt, black beanie hat against the grime. I don't know if he and the team were glad of a visitor, but their work was on schedule, and they were generous enough to indulge me for a couple of days.

We left the right whale hanging, in its sunlit window, and descended. The window space had been partitioned off to form a temporary workshop, a 'Laboratorium for HvalKonservering', which we passed through, then entered the Hvalsalen proper.

Without the natural light, the hall under the whale team's occupation was darker and more mysterious than before. It had taken on the temporary feel of a stage set. The glass display cases were shuttered with plywood; light from arc lamps glanced off scaffolding poles and caused the whales above to cast spooky shadows on the ceiling. About fifteen foot off the floor, a metal platform ran under the first three skeletons. From up there came voices, music, the sound of a vacuum cleaner being switched on, then off.

We passed the basking shark; it was wrapped in dust-sheets, and stalled in a sort of cave, it looked like a missile in a silo. Then Gordon led me to a different ladder, which led up through a trapdoor and onto the platform above. The platform was made of metal planks, and it ran back under the three biggest baleen whales, the ones nearest the door, the sei and humpback, side by side, then, nudging them along, the immense jaws of the blue whale itself. Beyond, yet to be reached, a crowd of others. In time, as the team worked on, the platform would be moved westward, a slow tide of cleanliness creeping over and through the whales.

The right whale, in its private space, was a shining destination, the 'after' in a colossal before-and-after task. For now, though, climbing that ladder was to enter into a strange lofty rag-and-bone shop, a beanstalk that entered into a kingdom of grime. It wasn't obvious from the floor just how much grease and dirt lay on the bones' upper sides. What, seen from below had seemed like the whales' stoicism, felt now like tremendous fatigue.

But they were working on it. Standing on either side of the sei whale's ribcage, as though grooming it, each with a stand of tools, and a vacuum cleaner between them, were Zina Fihl and Marielle Bergh, young women from Denmark and Sweden respectively. Zina pulled off her mask to greet me. Like Marielle, she wore workmen's clothes. Her blonde hair was tied back; she had a toothbrush poking from her overalls pocket, which made me smile.

'Tell me you're not cleaning a whale with a toothbrush . . .'

'Very important tool!' she laughed.

'Toothbrush!'

'Toothpick!'

'Cotton buds!'

'We tried dry ice and lasers, but they didn't work, so it's back to the household chemicals. Ammonia and ethanol, and a brush, and water and a sponge.'

I had two days. Zina loaned me some work clothes with padded knees and let me creep amongst the whales' skeletons. Sometimes we chatted as they worked; at other times I wandered in the gloom of the museum. Sometimes they were kind enough to show me things—for example, when the conversation turned to baleen, these all being baleen whales, Gordon asked me if I'd ever actually seen baleen. Aside from some ancient corset stays of my grandmother's, I hadn't, so he went to the store and returned with something which looked exactly like a shred of tyre, the kind of thing you see at the verge of the motorway if a lorry's had a blowout. It's made of the same stuff as our fingernails, and this piece was so hard you could knock on it, but in life, when the whale's mouth is constantly opening to the water, the baleen is soft, and frayed where the whale's huge tongue licks against it.

Being up on their platform, in the presence of these whales, allowed you to note differences in their anatomy, gave you a feel for them. It was as though you could imagine—purely by their skeletons hanging from their chains—differences in the characters they had in life. A kind of phrenology, I suppose, and probably meaningless, but the sei was regarded by all as an elegant creature. 'Feminine,' Zina called it, as she stroked the long slender ribs with a sponge. 'Gracile,' was Gordon's word. The sei's ribs were slim, more so than the right whale's and certainly more slender than the humpback's. The lowest ribs splayed wide and, though it's an odd word to use of a whale, they looked spidery; they almost wafted at the air, as if rowing it along.

Hanging beside the sei, the humpback was more a figure of fun. Thick-set—and filthy. In life humpbacks are characterful. They breach up out of the water, 'spy-hop' to see what's going on in the upper world, raise and slap their flippers—and there was a stocky robustness to this one's bones, in particular the scapulas. The humpback looked especially dirty, but its turn would come to be cleaned, 'Oh, he'll be quick,' they said. 'Then we'll get on to the blue.' For now, as he waited, the humpback was a useful shortcut. A rat run, you might say. To save bothering with ladders and trapdoors, to get across from one side of their platform to another, the conservators just crawled between the humpback's ribs into its chest cavity, then came stooping out of its belly, and carried on their way.

I'd learned from several quarters that the Hvalsalen was a bit of a mystery. There were few records, if any, of how the whales got to Bergen, or how they were prepared, or manoeuvred up the stairs, piece by piece presumably—if indeed they had been brought via the stairs at all—or how they were hoisted aloft, and chained to the ceiling.

A mystery, and Gordon had made a point to me that I reluctantly had to concede. It was when I'd been admiring the poor bright right whale. He'd said: 'I love bone, but you know what I also love? These chains.'

'Really?'

'Yes. I love metalwork, too. Archaeological metal, especially iron. And these chains—look at them! It's part of the thing—it's like the whales were giants that had to be restrained. They're all handmade—all handforged. We don't know much about how the whales got here, but there must have been a very good blacksmith on site. And the nails, see? All the metalwork that holds the skeletons together—everything's handmade. You couldn't do it now. The way I see it, this Hvalsalen is a monument to the whales—their only monument—but it's testament to those working men, too.'

I could see Gordon's point: they hung in monumental silence now, but each must had been a tremendous job of work, all fire and steam and the clang of the smith's hammer—dangerous, too. The Hvalsalen wasn't a big space. A blue whale within its confines was somewhat of a puzzle, like a ship in a bottle. But all the bolts and nails still looked Frankensteinian to me.

As to how they got there, though the records were scant, certain inferences could be drawn. Terje had said that the signs that hung from one or two whales, giving the dread dates 1867, 1879—dread in whale annals, that is—and the place, Finnmark—coincided with the invention of the exploding harpoon, and the opening of a whaling station there. Before that giant leap for humankind, fin whales had proved too fast to catch. But others may have been strandings. It happens.

Whether hunted or stranded, there was the nice question of how—or where—the whales had been eviscerated and defleshed. How and where they had been reduced to skeletons. There existed just one photograph, of a small whale laid on a cart outside the museum grounds. The gardens outside, with their pretty lily ponds, did seem the most likely place.

'How *would* you do it?'

We were standing next the sei whale, all fifty metres of it, the three conservators engaged in swabbing and brushing it down. Gordon gestured over to the humpback.

'Well, those look . . . *archaeological* to me. I mean, I think that one was buried. We could take samples; there would be traces of roots or soil, bacteriological signatures. As for the others . . . some might have been boiled.'

'In a huge tank?'

'Yes—they'd have made a tank specially. Cut off most of the flesh, then boiled the rest. And then, somehow, got them indoors and in here.'

Later, over tea, I asked the conservators if they thought of the objects they were working on as animals, or objects. 'Animals,' they said. They were all of a mind. Several times I heard the words 'waste' and 'slaughter' and 'holocaust' and 'shame'.

———————

Of course, when they said 'it's just glorified housework', the conservators were being disingenuous. How do you go about it? How do you go about cleaning twenty-four whale skeletons that have been hanging from a ceiling for a hundred and thirty years? It's bad enough spring-cleaning your bathroom.

'You appraise them. Look for problems, breakages, anything that needs repaired. You reconsider the old repairs and think if it can be done more sympathetically. Clean it all. Look again. Repair anything that needs repaired.'

Their work requires understanding of organic chemistry—
they were pretty sure that some of the old plaster had been
painted with lead-based paint, so they knew that would
be a problem to remove. The work also requires a craft-
worker's feel for materials and knowledge of how materials
respond to different conditions, how they decay and react
with air and each other. They used the word 'sympathetic',
too, as in 'a sympathetic repair'. They were concerned for
the future, about carrying things into the future in a fit
state. Sympathy and future concern, up amongst the great
dead whales.

They wouldn't only work with bone in their careers. At
one point Zina was seconded outdoors to advise on a flaky
stone lion.

I could understand the pleasures of the job. The near-
forensic task of working out what had happened in the past,
and the necessity to consider the future. The things we deem
worth keeping, that is, as we seem to be the arbiters of so
many fates. There are only 4000 blue whales alive now. At
the time of their deliverance, the moratorium of the 1960s,
we had slaughtered our way through 350,000.

The following morning I found Gordon occupied in the
workshop, the 'Laboratorium for HvalKonservering'. He
was grating a lump of cork with a metalworker's file.
Then he scraped the cork dust into a little pot. On the
desk lay a Kim's Game collection of objects: a compass, a
pot-scrubber, a ruler and a whale's rib, four foot long and
broken in two.

He said, 'I'm trying to find the best material to repair that bone with.'

'You're making a sort of Polyfilla?'

'But you'd never use Polyfilla—it's got calcium in it, so you'd never use it with bone. Someone coming along in the future has got to be able to tell what's original and what's repair, at a histological level.' Then he mixed the pot of cork dust he'd made with an adhesive called Paraloid. If it proved durable and flexible enough, he'd make sufficient to fill the cavity in the whale's rib.

'They're doing some sort of scientific work with them, the bones, aren't they? Dr Hufthammer mentioned it.'

I'd noticed on the sei whale's jaw that a hole had been bored, recently, as if someone had been at it with an apple-corer.

'Probably hoping to extract DNA samples, from a whale which lived before the "bottleneck". If they compare that to living whales' DNA, they can tell how much the gene pool has shrunk.'

A bottleneck is a biologists' term for when some catastrophe kills so many of a species of animal that only a few breeding pairs survive to repopulate the future. If they survive at all.

He mixed the potion with a wooden stick.

'Do they think the whales will ever really recover?'

Silly question, I suppose. They need clean, quiet, cold food-filled oceans, as well as each other. But you never stop hoping for silly answers. Like, 'Yes—it will all be fine. All manner of things shall be well.'

'Well, to put it indelicately, they don't hump much.' Gordon set aside his mix of cork and adhesive to go off.

'It's patient work . . .'
'Like all conservation work.'

I discovered that if I sat under the tremendous jaw of the blue whale, as if under an awning, I could watch what was going on across the hall without being in the way. The blue whale's jaw and the bone sheets of its palate were a source of fascination in themselves. There were many old repairs and interventions up there on the roof of its mouth, brown with age and too high to reach. A battery of tin-tacks marked where the baleen had been, because originally it was displayed, too—these tacks had held it in place—but insects had infested it sometime in the 1930s and it had been removed. There were wires, holding splits of bone together, and nails, and smears of gesso and splints of wood. I tried to concede Gordon's point about the artesans, but wherever in life there had been soft sinew or muscle or cartilage, now there was metal; what work the ocean had done in holding up the whale's bulk was done now by chains and rods. No one had gone so far as to carve their initials, but it had that feel, similar to an ancient tree, like everyone who encountered it had been challenged by it, had to leave some mark.

Two or three times on my visit I sat under the blue whale's jaw, or even within the cage of its chest, the thick portcullis of its ribs descending around. You got used to the scale, even to holding conversations in these surrounds. To sit within the creature's ribcage was like being in a very strange taxi, caught in traffic.

But you could conduct a bit of a thought experiment.

You could sit within the blue whale, and look back, following the spine with your eye as it voyaged above the hall, curving very slightly, continuing between the other whales, suspended every few yards by those chains and rods, until it tapered to an end far away. Then, of course, there would have been the tail, too, something the width of a small aircraft. Despite the size, you could, with a minimum of effort, extend your sense of self, and imagine this was your body, moving through the ocean. You could begin to imagine what it might feel like, to be a blue whale.

I sat there, as the others worked, and wished, as I often do, that I could draw. I'd draw the great sculptural shapes and shadows that arced over me and round, the honed shapes of the 'spinous process' marching away. I'd draw scenes like the war artists did, especially the appropriately named Muirhead Bone, whose war drawings show figures up on gantries working on fuselages bigger than themselves. Of course, this was a smaller scale, but to watch the conservation team reaching and kneeling, in workmen's clothes and masks, moving around the crates of the whales, gave something of the same idea.

I was lurking in the blue whale's chest on my second afternoon. Marielle and Zina were at their stations at the sei whale, when Gordon, released from a meeting, came up the ladder and passed by, but as he did, something caught his attention.

'Look, there's a fracture!' he said, and entered into the creature's belly, and ran his hand down a rib on the whale's left. The rib thickened at a place two-thirds down, then thinned again. 'That's been broken there, and healed.'

'Wonder what did that.'

'Who knows. Perhaps they fight. Maybe it hit a ship.'

'It would take a lot to break a whale's rib, wouldn't it?' I said. 'I mean, inside all the blubber?'

'But it would deliver a shockwave . . . and look at this side—see these scrapes on this rib here? This one's been flensed . . .'

Of course it became ridiculous only to watch others and ask questions. Housework? I could do that.

Marielle and Zina, voices muffled by the masks they were wearing against the ammonia, were still at work on the sei whale—as they would be for some time yet.

I called over. 'Can I help?'

'We thought you'd never ask! Come on—let's get you a mask.'

I crawled through the humpback's ribs toward them, and found Marielle sitting under the humpback's spine with a sei rib across her lap. They'd undone some bolt or other and taken it off, the better to clean it. There was another waiting attention, too. So I sat beside her, cross legged with a sei whale rib arcing my lap too, a piece of evolutionary work curved and honed, with a slight kink to it, and a club-like thickness at the end.

Marielle showed me what to do. First, you spray your rib with ammonia from a plastic bottle, then you take a brush, the kind you'd use for the washing-up, and work the ammonia onto the rib, working into the grain. Then you wipe it down with a sponge, simple, and at once a layer of dark dirt comes away. The bone emerges lighter and brighter. This is gratifying.

Marielle, her long red hair tied back, with her rib; me with mine. Zina standing on the far side of the whale, occasionally switching on and off a vacuum cleaner, played it along the spine.

It was the quiet lull of mid-afternoon. We talked a little. Marielle was writing her university master's dissertation on the collection. She was the one poring over the old museum records and daybooks, trying to put together something of the history of the Hvalsalen. She cleaned bones by day and in the evenings sought clues as to how they got there.

'They're in Norwegian, aren't they, the records?'

'Yes, but I can read them, aside for a few words.'

She had worked in museums in London, and told me her dream job would be to go to the Antarctic, to help conserve Scott's hut.

I suppose we could have been housemaids, set to polish the silverware in some mansion, except for being high above the floor, with a whale crowd around us. It was quite absorbing. We worked into the stubborn parts of our respective bones and, indeed, toothpicks were provided, to winkle out hardened little deposits of gunk. Soon, it would be the humpback's turn, then the blue whale's.

The blue whale, awaiting the attention of the toothpick. Then, they'd have taken everything we could throw at them. The full gamut of human attention—from the exploding harpoon and flensing iron, to the soft sponge and the toothpick.

Gordon came up the ladder, said was pleased with his reconstituted cork. It would be flexible enough and strong enough to fill the cavities in the right whale's broken rib.

The sound of the young women's voices and the brushes. The whales' otherworldly presence.

'Ever seen a whale?' I asked Marielle. 'Alive, I mean?'

'No! None of us has. We were talking about this just the other day. We really should try; we spend all day with them here . . .'

'You get such a feel for them, don't you think? All their differences. Different species, different characters?'

'I would love to see a whale . . .'

'We should go together,' said Zina. 'Whale-Teambuilding!'

'Oh, you should!' I said. 'Really—find a way. Of course, all you see is a blow, a back, a fin or tail. To have to imagine all this . . .'

I watched as she turned the rib in her gloved hand, appraising it.

'That's coming up nicely.' There is some old magic to do with cleaning bones. Something ancient and fairy story. Something prehistoric, maybe. All those chambered cairns piled with clean bones.

The end of her rib rested on a cushion of foam so it wouldn't be damaged. 'Do not touch the animals'! Sometimes our species beggars belief.

I scooshed some more ammonia onto mine, sponged it off again. All across the hall, the crowd of whales waited their turn for treatment, huge and otherworldly. Not otherworldly. Actually, *of* this world, as they had been for a very long time, long before we appeared.

I turned the rib in my hands, stroked it with the sponge. Shame and shame.

'How clean does it have to be, Marielle?'

All unwitting, I'd asked the conservator's question of questions. She just smiled.

MOON

_____

Only a barbarian mind
could fail to see the flower,
only an animal mind
could fail to dream a moon

—BASHO

HIGH OVER THE TOWN'S PITCHED ROOFS and chim-
neys: the full moon. By now her pewtery, equivalising light
would be falling on the whole night-bound world. I leaned
out of the attic window; through binoculars the moon was
stunning, filling my field of vision. There's a line from a
poem by Elizabeth Bishop: 'He does not see the moon; he
observes only her vast properties'. To think of all those moon
songs, all that poetry; centuries' worth of idle dreamers and
parted lovers, gazing at the full moon, before aeroplanes,
satellites, text messaging.

That evening we'd received two phone calls and a text
message. One call was from my father, reading out a note

from the newspaper; another from friends inviting us to their house, where they had a telescope. We were all reminding each other of the imminent eclipse. Not only would the night be dark—it was March—but it promised to be clear.

Because my own children had friends staying over, we declined the invitation, and instead urged the children to come and look through the window and see what was happening. The two boys were leaping around the living room making whooping noises, but the two girls, my daughter and her friend, were snuggled close together on the sofa, playing with Nintendos. Each girl gazed at her own silvery screen. 'Come and see the moon,' I said. 'Later,' they said. I went back upstairs alone.

———

When the shadow first began to creep onto the moon's face, it was translucent, like black silk. Its leading edge was convex. As it moved very slowly up onto the shining face of the moon it emphasised, rather than obscured, the texture of her surface; under the shadow, the lunar seas and craters were, if anything, more clearly etched than before. I watched through the open windows, alternating between the binoculars and my own eye. I had to kneel, to get the angle right. If you looked long enough, you could actually see the shadow move. At least, it appeared that way—as though the shadow was moving, not the moon. I suppose that was an illusion. The room behind me was dark, with no electric lights on. From downstairs, the children's voices; they were quite happy to be staying up late, ignored by adults. The leading edge of the shadow was green.

There was something unnerving about the movement of this shadow or, rather, about the passivity of the moon. She couldn't wipe or shake away the encroaching shadow. She had no option but to accept what was befalling her. Of course, that's a fine example of the pathetic fallacy. A moon can neither accept nor decline. Here was the earth's shadow and she had to enter into it, inevitably; the moon is only a rock. But, as when a friend goes into labour, or a crisis, or has to undergo some procedure, it's concerning. I was watching the moon with growing unease, and meanwhile thinking that I ought to go downstairs and fetch the children to look at this grand lunar event, and then usher them into bed. But I didn't. More time passed, half an hour or so. Of course time passed. As the shadow crept onward, upward, smooring the moon's light as it went, I half understood that what I was watching *was* time, at least by my simple understanding of it. What is time to us mortals, if not the succession of nights and days, months and years, and what is that if not the collusion of sun and earth and moon? In watching the shadow cover the moon, I was watching time pass. When the moon's lower two-thirds were in shadow, the upper third, as yet free, seemed to shine extra brightly in response.

The windows overlook the back gardens, then the land rises into a low hill, so there are few intruding lights in that direction. The hill was quite dark now against the night sky, and the curve of its brow was almost exactly the same arc as the shadow on the moon. I didn't know why the shadow creeping over the moon should be curved, rather than straight, but presumed it was to do with the curvature

of the earth. I love that phrase 'the curvature of the earth'—
it denotes a fabled thing, visible, they say, from the crow's
nest of a ship. Whatever the reason, it pleased me to think
that from my own house, with the children messing about
downstairs, where the telly was switched on but ignored
and the dog lay curled in his basket, I could appreciate the
curvature of the earth. Indeed, could appreciate the earth as
an astronaut would, as a heavenly body. Mostly, if I think of
it at all, it's as an indigene, a participant in its general daily
melee.

Of course I'd seen the Apollo 11 pictures of the blue
planet suspended in space, but they made Earth look
homely. However, this shadow arching across the moon's
bright face, right now in front of my eyes, was dark, stately
and solemn. The moon does us great service, metaphorically
and literally, and this is part of it—occasionally she allows
us to appreciate the shadow cast by our own planet. She
shows us that the earth, for all the cacophony of life on its
surface, is firstly an object, bigger than we are, magisterial
enough to cast a shadow thousands and thousands of miles
into space. The earth-shadow, a long and empty cone, falls
on nothing, until every few months the moon swims into
its ken.

By now the moon's lower right side, the westward side,
had taken on a reddish blush, like the blush on the skin of
a fruit. As the moon moved farther into the earth's shadow,
this red blush deepened in colour. I kept watching, shifting
from one window to the other. It was as though the moon
was ripening, quickly, as plums do. By its shadow, the earth
had been revealed as massive and mineral, but the lifeless

moon, on entering into that shadow, was changing colour. It looked as though it was becoming less barren, more like a living thing. Further, because the reddish coloration of the moon's lower side deepened as it curved away out of sight, it showed that the moon was a sphere. No longer a silver plate hung in the sky, the moon was turning into a bruised ball. The moon was a sphere. It sounds obvious, but I had just never seen it before.

The reddish blush intensified. I couldn't leave it now.

At its top, the moon's glow was reduced to a desperate sliver. As it darkened and reddened in this way, it looked as though the moon was undergoing some Ovidian metamorphosis, ceasing to be mineral and becoming vegetable, or more, farther, pushing on through vegetable into animal. It looked as though the moon was becoming a body, as though she were one of those gods who want to stop looking down on us all, and instead participate, at least for a while; who want to taste the mutability of earthly existence.

Now the whole of the moon was painted with coppery reds, weal-reds. They were mammalian colours, the shades of an incarnation, colours liable to pain. Isn't this what great paintings tell us? That to take the form of flesh, the form of a body, is difficult, vulnerable, and yet—perhaps because of that—sweetly enviable. Here was the moon becoming fruit, or flesh; she looked like the one fruit in a vanitas painting, the one soft globe among the peaches and pomegranates which is already beginning to darken toward decay.

A dog barked, a quarter of a mile way. A few geese were passing, calling as they went. Did the moon's transformation discomfit them? Could they notice, with their animal minds? Would I have noticed myself, come to that, being so caught up in the general melee, had my dad not called and the neighbour not called, had the friend not sent his text message. The earth, a fizzing ball of telephony and messaging bringing this news: look out tonight, we'll see our own shadow falling on the face of the moon. I called the kids, and this time they all came bundling up into the dark attic, all wanting to look through the binoculars. The children's dark heads bobbed and ducked as they took turns to look at the red moon, and the boys explained to each other loudly what was happening. 'Cool!' they said. 'Brilliant!'

Then a smirr of cloud drifted across. Cloud is not like shadow: it passes like a silly thing, without the shadow's cold deliberation. Under the drift of cloud the remaining moonlight and the colours were abolished and the moon was a disc beaten into the sky like a rivet, horrible and annulled. Then the cloud passed.

That was six weeks ago. Since then I've given the moon no more than a glance. Tonight, though, I'm looking at the moon again, this time from the cabin of an aeroplane. Mine is a window seat, right over the wing. The plane is travelling above a field of cloud which ripples softly all the way to the eastern horizon, and there, above the rippling sea of cloud, the moon hangs as though from a peg.

We've been airborne for about ninety minutes, so I'd guess we're somewhere over Canada, the Bay of Fundy maybe, already swinging east for the dart across the Atlantic, toward the dawn. I'm travelling with a friend who's scared of flying; during takeoff he clutched my hand and only let go, mumbling an apology, when the plane levelled off. He's still scared, and just wishes it to be over. I want to tell him that, like the lights of New York City that blazed below us for ages, livid and thrilling, taking off in a 747 is the business—truly the modern sublime. We *should* be terrified, or awestruck, but he's in no mind to listen to my philosophising. It's the woman next to him who fixed a sleep-mask over her eyes, even before the plane began to taxi, or the man across the aisle who read his paper, or purported to, as the plane banked over the city—they're the ones who should be ashamed. 'At least you know you're alive,' I tell my friend, but he just gives me a wild look in return.

Now drinks have been served, the cabin lights are dimmed, the little video monitors above our heads are showing *Casino Royale*, but I can't concentrate on that. I'd sooner cup my hands round my eyes and look out the window. The plane's wing is pointing directly toward the yellow moon, although the moon seems to hang at a lower altitude than the wing-tip. I say 'seems to', because, as with the moving shadow of the eclipse, I don't know what is actual and what is illusory, or if this matters. I realise that sometimes I call the moon 'it', sometimes 'she'—both are apposite, and this doesn't matter, either.

Tonight she is in her first quarter, at the edge of the night sky, golden and opulent as a honeycomb. The night we travel through is flooded with her light. I watch her, but because she's screened by cloud from the world below I feel I've intruded on a privacy. During the eclipse, she'd seemed briefly to be taking on the colours of a body, but now she's

restored to herself, bright and mineral again. We're the em-
bodied ones, the ones of woman born, and what do we do
but throw ourselves round the world in aeroplanes, railing
against the constraints of earthly existence, of gravity, fini-
tude, distance, dark.

In a minute I'll offer to swap seats with my friend so
he can observe the moon's vast properties, and be calmed.
Her light gilds the leading edge of the plane's wing. The
engines drone steadily. The wing-lights beat like a heart.

THREE WAYS OF LOOKING AT ST KILDA

———

1.

A GOOD FEW YEARS AGO NOW, when the children were small and the world had shrunk to the here and now, I was taken with the notion to go to St Kilda. Cliff-ridden and bird-wreathed—and totally unlikely, on the whole. There were days back then when even the post office seemed an unwinnable shore.

But that was the point. I'd been kneeling on the carpet, putting Lego away and wondering: which was the closest place one could go that was remote? Where an adventure could unfold—just enough to keep one's wits sharp, enough to let one taste an untamed grandeur, yet be back in a few days because, you know, of the children? I mean, everyone wants to escape their own lives sometimes, don't they?

As I say, that was some years ago now. A time when everything had become immediate and small: small people and toy cities built of wooden blocks. Toy boats sailing the living-room floor.

It was arranged. As a fortieth birthday present I would go to St Kilda, and be gone a week. I'd go west of the Hebrides, way over the horizon, and my husband would look after the kids.

———————

The St Kilda story is like a modern myth and, like a myth, I can't remember when I first heard it. Possibly in primary school. One afternoon we were shown a film. Barefoot, bearded men, and women cowled in shawls, and innumerable seabirds filled the screen. There were dreadful cliffs that the men lowered themselves down, to take birds' eggs and the birds themselves. We learned that the islands lay forty miles west of Lewis and Harris, out in the ocean, which was too far for much contact or communication, in those days. Nonetheless, people had lived out there for a thousand years or more. They grew a few crops and kept a strange kind of wild sheep, and they ate seabirds, and seabirds' eggs. They made shoes out of gannets and medicine out of fulmar oil; they stitched their clothes with feathers.

But their way of life broke on the wheel of the modern world. The nineteenth century brought steamships, and Victorian tourists from the industrial cities, already enamoured of 'remoteness'. The young ones' heads were turned; they couldn't get the things they'd learned to want, they began to emigrate, until it all became impossible, and in 1930 the few remaining St Kildans asked to be evacuated. Their peat fires were extinguished and their islands left to the birds. That's what we learned. Eventually, the islands were handed over to the National Trust for Scotland, who now have the uneasy task of 'managing' the fabled island, and preserving it, as more and more people want to see it for themselves.

It was thrilling to be aboard a yacht for the first time, to feel the swoop of the sea and stand on the spray deck in the wind. Aside from the skipper, Donald Wilkie, we were five paying passengers thrown together for the trip, and we included two elderly Germans, a couple who, it became apparent, were perfectly fixated on St Kilda. How the reputation of St Kilda had reached north-central Europe I never found out, but suspect it followed the highway of romance laid down by Ossian and Walter Scott. The German couple were candid about it—the man was ill, and wanted to experience wild, abandoned St Kilda and all its birds, before it was too late.

But the sea was dark and gurly. The first night we anchored at the low-lying Monach Islands, where the boat fretted in the wind. The radio brought forecast after forecast of deteriorating weather. At last Donald leaned over the chart-desk and said, 'I don't think we can go.'

'Because of the wind?'

'It's backing east and rising. You heard. You don't want to be at St Kilda in an east wind. No, we can't go.'

The boat rocked. Soon he would move to another, safer anchorage. The conversation was in English. Slow translations were made.

'We don't go to St Kilda?' exclaimed the German woman.
Donald shook his head.

'But we must go!'

Again there was a pause, a tense one this time.

'What do you think?' he said to me. We were sitting
down in the yacht's saloon, around a table. Above, the wind
in the shrouds rose to a shriek.

'I just live down the road,' I said. 'I can come again.
Anyway, you're the skipper.'

'Oh, yes. I'm the boss.' He laughed.

At the end of the week, as though Donald felt he had let
us down, he said, 'We couldn't have gone, you know.'

'It's alright,' I replied.

'Sailors dread an east wind in Village Bay. It can cut off
your escape, even drive you onshore . . . but some of them
are fixated on it. A fantasy!'

'Who?'

'The people who charter my yacht! St Kilda! Oh, they've
read the maps, studied all the books, know the place better
than I do—and I've been going there twenty years.'

'You mean, people who've never been there?'

'It's like the Holy Grail. The edge of the world. That's
what they come looking for. It's what they've heard about
and nothing else will do.'

That's what I'd wanted myself. Sea-cliffs and abandonment. The last adventure. But I kept quiet. We were anchored in the most beautiful cliff-backed bay. The boat
turned softy as the tide ebbed. Above the darkling cliff
shone a single star.

But, actually, it must be pretty wild and remote out

there, I thought, if we didn't even catch sight of the place, if the wind and weather kept us firmly away.

'There was a time when you could rely on the weather in May,' said Donald, as though he'd read my mind. 'But you can't now.'

But it's an ill wind that blows no one any good. Had we headed straight out of harbour, reached St Kilda and spent our time there, I'd never have known the places Donald revealed to us instead. We had adventures enough, landing in the dinghy in a swell. There were plenty other wild shores to explore. And people—because nowhere is truly wild or abandoned, we met a few shepherds and fishermen. I could let the soft local accent fall on my ears.

What became of the elderly Germans I don't know, except that they went home disappointed. I headed home, too, determined to know more about the places that lay almost on my doorstep.

I'd been on the desert islands, my husband had been at home with the infants. He was the one who looked ravaged, like Robinson Crusoe.

2.

A couple of years later and a lad driving home from his job at a fish farm kindly went out of his way to deliver me to Berneray's tiny harbour where the *Annag* waited, under its tall mast, as before. I'd hitched from the ferry terminal, it was already late in the Hebridean evening. This time we were just three—skipper Donald, and his colleague Iain, who was to act as mate.

'Look at this,' Donald said, and held out an oblong of black plastic the size of a domino. It was almost too small for his fingers to manipulate. He slotted it into a slot on a new instrument above the chart desk. A small green screen lit up, and the yacht appeared as a blinking cursor among contour lines.

'There are fourteen charts on that little bit of plastic. Imagine! Trouble is, I find myself staying down here looking at screens. I deplore it in other sailors—it's the sea you should be watching, not a screen, but these days I'm doing it myself.'

Next morning we put out from Berneray. As before it was dull, the sea steel-grey. Iain steered the yacht between flat green islands through the Sound, then we were out beyond the Hebrides, sailing due west. It was looking good, but Donald said, 'We might not be able to get there, you know . . .'

'Oh, I'm aware of that!'

'But the forecast's not bad. The wind's veering southwest.'

'Really,' I said. 'There are other places.'

'Oh, I know there are other places. Wonderful places, but oh no—everyone wants to go to St Kilda. You want to go to St Kilda.'

By afternoon we were out of sight of land, doing about seven knots, with the sails rising into an overcast sky. Iain was on watch, in his red waterproofs. Iain was Hebridean, an engineer. I liked his calm presence, his measured Gaelic speaker's accent. The skipper was in his cabin, resting. Unlike myself, scared to miss a moment of the sea's nothingness, the skipper and mate were assiduous in their resting, because they never knew when they might have to stay up all night.

At length Donald came up into the cockpit, into the wind and light. He glanced at the compass, glanced under the sail at the horizon and, following some thought of his own, said, 'You know, mariners have always known the earth was round.' Then, to me: 'Do you want to take watch? Why don't you take an hour's watch and call me at three. Iain can rest.'

'Watch for what?'

'Anything. Other vessels. Objects in the water, anything. And whales. Call me if you see any whales.'

He swung downstairs again, Iain followed. The yacht followed its preordained course and I was alone in the buffeting wind.

How rarely we stand still for an hour, watching. I say 'stand still' but there was a constant bracing and relaxing, a whooping in the belly as the boat pitched. I stood on a step behind the wheel, head to toe in waterproofs against the spray and, clinging to a wire, watched earnestly, like a child charged with a great task. But there was nothing to see but the sea. On all sides: waves, under a grey mist, and the sails. The sea took its chance to play tricks. Waves became just too bright and edgy, as though I'd taken some mild hallucinogen. Many times I rubbed my eyes. Other vessels. Objects in the water. Nothing broke the surface. No whales, but there were gannets passing alongside, necks outstretched. It was exciting to see them, to know they were intent on the same place as we were. Riding on the waves were rafts of guillemots, now visible as they crested, now lost in the troughs.

Later in the afternoon four or five spikes of land appeared across a grey sea. Iain was on watch by then, and I kneeled in the cockpit. Ever more birds passed alongside, and St Kilda was defining itself as we neared. It should have been thrilling, except that by then I was throwing up into an orange plastic bucket. In the long fetch between bouts of vomiting, I could see that each island was tall and mysterious, and capped in its own private cloud. When he saw me looking, Iain shouted the litany of the islands' names: 'That's Hirta! That's Stac Lee. That one's Boreray. Stac an Armin.'

And then we sailed slowly into a deep bay, Village Bay, surrounded by high hills. Puffins scuttered over the surface ahead of the yacht, or dived away. But the cloud was down, a dank sort of cloud that obscured the island. Hills, smooth, treeless, khaki-coloured, with scree slopes, rose a few hundred feet, then was mist. There was a jetty and, on the shore, left of that, some flat-roofed prefabricated buildings which gave the place an air of desolation. A curious line, like the strand line of a very high tide, scratched along the hill-foot, then petered out halfway round the bay. I realised with a start that that was the famous village itself, the forlorn, abandoned street.

Iain came and stood beside me and together we looked at this sorry outpost as the boat rocked. For a minute neither of us spoke. Then he said, 'Do you know, in Gaelic there is a phrase: *"Nach du bha'n a Hirst!"*—"I wish you were on Hirta!" You say it when you want rid of someone.'

'Kilda ranger!' said the radio, brashly, making me jump. It was a young man with an English public school accent. 'Rainjah', he pronounced it, through the radio's fizz. 'Kildah rainjah, just wanted to know if you intend to come ashore?'

Iain had said that Hebridean people don't come out here now. His own swift Gaelic phrase would be the only words of the native language I'd hear.

The ranger was waiting alone on the damp concrete jetty to greet us. A cheerful young man with binoculars round his neck, he said he was employed by the National Trust for Scotland, and was new to the post. He'd been there three weeks. He was welcoming, but he was obliged to read some bylaws.

'Been here before?' he asked. Donald was kicking stones, as though to indicate he'd been coming here since this lad was in his pram. The warden duly warned against harming birds' nests or removing artefacts or jumping on walls or damaging anything, anything, anything at all.

'There's a little shop I'll open for you if you like. Cottage four is a museum; just go in. Staying tonight? Maybe see you in the Puff Inn later, for a drink . . .'

The warden turned and headed back along the jetty and up a grassy slope toward the assortment of prefabs. No one else seemed to be around.

'What is all that?' I asked Donald, nodding toward the buildings.

'The radar base, of course! The missile-tracking base! Some people are horrified by it. Remember I told you how some folk have got this romantic idea of St Kilda? What do they get? A radar base. Wardens and bylaws. A souvenir shop.'

Donald was untying the dinghy, ready to go back out to his yacht, which rocked back and forth, tall and white in the bay. The plan was that I'd have an hour or so, then we'd eat on the yacht, then come ashore again, and tomorrow and tomorrow to explore, really to be on St Kilda.

And that was pretty well that. The island was semi-conscious under a peculiar, oppressive atmosphere; cloud like damp wool obscured its hills. Of the village I saw nothing but a chaos of stone, or what looked like chaos. In the little museum were nineteenth-century photographs of bearded men assembled in the village street, and women sitting on the ground, preparing to pluck a mound of dead fulmars. I looked at those, then wandered back to the jetty. Snipe called, and I heard waves and the drone of the diesel generator. No matter, I thought, maybe the cloud would clear. There would be tomorrow for all the breathtaking clifftop views.

Donald didn't say much as I clambered down from the jetty. The yacht was rolling hard, though the saloon smelled wonderfully of moussaka.

'Told you the good news, has he?' called Iain, from the stove.

'What's that?'

'We can't stay. The coastguard's just issued a revised weather forecast.'

'Revised . . . ?'

'As in, contradicting this morning's one. East winds. We've got to leave.'

Donald ate in silence. After seven straight hours' sailing, he was looking at another seven hours back again, through the night, in worsening weather. He ate, then pushed his plate aside and went to attend to the anchor, saying, 'It's the forecast, and we've got to act on it.'

'Ach well,' said Iain. 'Maybe it's better to see St Kilda this way.'

'What way?'

'Fleetingly!'

They laughed when I got home. Wild, remote, famous, oft-imagined St Kilda, so theatrically abandoned . . . Did you get there? Yup, but not for long. In fact, I've spent longer standing at bus stops.

3.

Two or three years passed. There were, as Donald had so rightly said, other places, wonderful places. During that time, something unforeseen began to happen. Through my work, and in the way of small countries, my path began to cross with those of other people engaged with, familiar with, such places. People who'd began as I had, scruffing around lonely shores in their teens, but were older now, and who had even made careers of it: naturalists, archaeologists, artists. I was welcomed into a group of friends whose winter conversations were always planning sessions. As the new kid, I heard a lot of derring-do and anecdotes. I had to bone up on history, and quickly learned the names of islands and lighthouses and birds and boatmen, especially boatmen, because none of us could sail. There were maps and charts to pore over. Who could take us where, and when? We spoke of the fabled outliers, St Kilda, North Rona, Sula Sgeir; of gannets and puffin colonies and bothies and brochs; we drew up shopping lists of pasta and instant custard. Over the next few years we made summer trips to the nearer but depopulated places: Mingulay, Pabbay, Stroma, the Shiant Isles. Places with such long human histories, I soon came to distrust any starry-eyed notions of 'wild' or 'remote'. Remote from what? London? But what was London?

I pinned the sea chart—a paper one, not the tiny plastic domino of the autopilot—on the wall of my room at the university. Few students gave the chart a second glance, and fair enough. At their age, and without responsibilities, they wanted the bright lights and adventures that were truly far away. But one day I came in early and found the cleaner in her blue overalls, Hoover at her feet, studying the chart closely. She was a smart and lively woman about my age. We spoke for a while about places we'd like to go. What surprised her, she said, was everything else the chart disclosed: firing ranges, tanker lanes, lights and beacons, submarine exercise areas. She pointed to the smudge of islands farthermost west. 'St Kilda,' said Liz. 'I'd love to go there.'

I told her how it had eluded me and she laughed, saying, 'It wouldn't be the same if everything ran to a timetable, would it?' Indeed no. But whenever I saw pictures of the abandoned street, or the great gannet colonies, whenever I heard my friends talking of St Kilda, it rankled with me. I said I hankered to go to Rona, too, which lies so far in the north I had to stand on a chair to show Liz where it was.

Then, one winter's day, in Edinburgh, I met my new friend Jill Harden for lunch. Jill is an archaeologist who worked then for the National Trust for Scotland. She was often on St Kilda, to my chagrin, and she'd laughed when I'd told her my 'fleeting' tale. But she had something up her sleeve.

Over our lunch—I believe mine grew cold on the plate— Jill told me that, in the coming May, a party of surveyors from RCAHMS—the Royal Commission on Ancient and Historical Monuments of Scotland—would be going to St

Kilda to begin a big project. Over several visits across three years they intended to plot the entire 'cultural landscape' of the archipelago. Every last man-made structure on the islands would be surveyed with the latest GPS satellite equipment.

'It's because it's a World Heritage Site. Really, they're bringing Mary Harman's work up to date.'

I must have looked blank, because Jill went on to tell me that in the late 1970s a pioneering archaeologist called Mary Harman had gone to St Kilda. She had been the first to appreciate that, when they left, the St Kildan people had left behind a complete expression in stone of a unique way of life—a way of life that had lasted centuries. Maybe longer. Maybe thousands of years. Working alone, and in gruelling conditions, Mary Harman had compiled the first record of the islands' structures.

Jill went on. 'You know the army wanted to bulldoze the village?'

'Bulldoze it?'

'In the 1950s, when they built the radar base. You know the road that goes up the hill?'

Again I shook my head. In my fleeting visit I'd barely seen the hills, never mind a road.

'Well, they wanted to bulldoze the village and put the road there. You can see their point. No one lived there any more.'

'But they were dissuaded?'

'And now it's a World Heritage Site.'

The first trip would last a fortnight. Jill was going with the surveyors in her professional capacity, to assist and advise. She said there might well be space on the motorboat, which was being chartered specially. There would certainly be space in the 'Ladies' Boudoir'—one of the old cottages now reroofed and turned into a dormitory, more usually used by volunteer work parties. She said if I petitioned in the right quarters and offered to pay my costs, I might well be in luck.

———

We left Harris one blustery blue morning in early May and this time the journey was fast and direct: three hours' sail due west, if 'sail' is the word, in a powerful motorboat that left a straight wake over the water. Noise and salt winds and spray, and soon, like raised wings, the extravagant St Kilda cliffs again appeared on the horizon.

It was exciting, but I was glad to have made the journey before, more slowly, by yacht; to have gained some small sense of the distance and seas people endured in the olden days of open boats. Else you might think—what was the problem?

When the boat engines cut, the silence seemed preternatural. Then there were birdcalls, and waves washing on the shore, and the same low anonymous buildings of the base. I could follow with my eye the trickle of ruins, house after roofless house, brown hills bearing down on them. Everything that day was sunlit, the sky high and pelagic. Then it was a matter of hefting ashore all the surveyors' equipment: out of the hold and into the dinghy came strongboxes containing satellite receivers, laptops, batteries, chargers and digital cameras—the wherewithal of the scientific gaze.

And a fortnight's worth of food, plus extra, in case we were stormbound.

I liked the four RCAHMS surveyors at once. Three men and a woman, they were robust, friendly people well used to fieldwork in faraway places. A lot of good-natured banter passed between them. They'd a deep knowledge of their country, but none had been to St Kilda before. That's why Jill had come, and waiting on the jetty to greet us was another archaeologist, a young New Zealander called Sam Dennis. Like Jill, Sam worked for the National Trust for Scotland. She was spending the whole summer here on St Kilda. The whole group would make up two teams to do the survey work, two surveyors and an archaeologist in each.

We jolted all the gear up to the village in wheelbarrows: the valuable equipment, the coffee and bananas and potatoes and bread. May sunshine poured down between fast-moving clouds. Third time lucky! Whenever we passed each other, manoeuvring our wheelbarrows, Jill caught my eye and smiled. Little gangs of brown lambs ran about; they were of the wild, indigenous breed called Soay sheep. Across the steep-sided bay, there turned a constant carousel of puffins.

That evening, when everything was unpacked and the surveyors had checked and accounted for all their equipment, all the cables and leads, and every electrical socket in the common room had a laptop or battery pack attached to it, we all went for a stroll around town. Sam the archaeologist had offered to show us the village, and suggest why, after many centuries, life on St Kilda had come suddenly to an end. This was a brave move—when it came to 'historical monuments', she was an expert among experts. It was a slow walk: everyone had to pore over everything. We moved along the gaunt parade of roofless cottages, glancing through the gaps where the doors had been. Nettles and thistles grew out of their cold hearths.

Even I could see the cottages were pretty ordinary, architecturally speaking, like you'd find all over the country. What excited the surveyors were the buildings called cleits—*cleitean* in Gaelic, with a Scots 'ch' in the middle, though English speakers just say 'cleits', to rhyme with 'meets'.

Sam led us behind the cottages, to the area confined within a long head-dyke, and we gathered by a particularly handsome example: a head-height oval building, made of drystone, which corbelled in a little, and was roofed with living turf. At one end was a low, dark, oracular doorway. It looked like a Neolithic Andersen shelter. That was the point, really. These buildings, unique to St Kilda, could have been prehistoric, or could have been built just before the people left.

'That's the problem here,' Sam laughed ruefully. 'The Stone Age went on till 1930!'

Cleits were stores. In the days when St Kilda was wholly remote and self-sufficient, these cleits had held grain, snared seabirds, seabirds' eggs, peats: all the resources that stood between the people and privation. There seemed to be dozens around the village and, once you got your eye in, all over the hill, too—lumps and bumps on the upper slopes, like buttons holding down the land against the wind.

We looked at cleits, we looked at the well. We examined prehistoric mounds, we looked at enclosures and the wallheads of old blackhouses—those thatched and window-less buildings that were standard peasant homes. Then we were back on the street, so we glanced round the museum with its photographs of bearded, barefoot men, of shy, shawled women. Then Sam led us further along pavement, house after house. She wanted to say something about the evacuation, about why, after so long, St Kilda had become untenable.

Part of the reason was these ordinary cottages, the famous, much-photographed, 'street' itself.

'It was "aid", as we'd now say,' she explained. 'Early in the nineteenth century a wealthy Englishman had come here, a tourist if you like, and he'd been appalled at the islanders' traditional blackhouses.'

Blackhouses were nothing unusual—they were common all over the highlands and islands in those days. Thatched and windowless, with a central hearth and a space for the animals at one end, they were hardly luxurious, but they worked.

'So, this man pledged money to encourage the people to build better houses—"better" in his eyes—with a chimney for the smoke, and glass windows, and a separate byre for the beasts.' The then minister encouraged the scheme and so did the laird and, by 1860, these cottages were the result. Modern, mainland-style they may have been, but they were not an improvement. They were damp and needy.

'He thought he was doing them a favour, but these new houses had windows. If the glass broke, well, where do you get window glass, here? They needed paint . . . timber . . . but how d'you get timber where there's no trees . . . ?'

Sam gestured out into the bay, in the direction of the faraway mainland cities and then burgeoning factories.

'That was the beginning of the end. Seventy years later, everyone was gone.'

Next morning, laden with rucksacks full of equipment and spare clothes, because the weather could turn on a sixpence, and carrying metal strongboxes with the more delicate equipment, we passed along the street and, when it petered out, crossed a damp hillside and a burn, then picked up the army road Jill had spoken of, which climbs the thousand feet up onto the heights of the island. The road connects the base with a collection of white-domed radar buildings that face the Atlantic on a promontory, and which, the surveyors pointed out, feature on no map. Once you were high, breathless on the hillcrest, though, if you turned your back on those, the modern world vanished. Village Bay, the base, the abandoned houses and village cleits were all out of sight, and at the top of the hill we were on a scant two miles of high hinterland that looked like birds had designed it for themselves. Everywhere was flight and fall, tilted rock and ramparts, a few turf slopes and sheer cliffs to breed on, and no need of anything else.

The surveyors divided into two teams of two, each with an archaeologist. The most senior of the surveyors was Ian Parker, a gentle, knowledgeable man. He and his colleague Adam Welfare would be working with Sam and they intended to make their way along the edge called Mullach Mor, a southwest-facing clifftop from where the land sloped steeply 800 feet down to the sea. The rock ramparts and tremendous sea-views attracted me, so I asked to tag along with them. As Sam nimbly led the way, in single file they carried the rucksacks and boxes along little paths the wild sheep made. To the left, the sea was too far below for its sound to reach us. It was breeding time, so a constant traffic of birds swirled around the island; every tiny gleam over the sea was a bird. Gannets, from the great gannetries of Stac an Armin and Stac Lee, four sea miles north, and silent fulmars and arrow-lines of guillemots. There were bonxies, too, nesting on the short turf. You had to watch out for them, these great skuas. If they didn't like the cut of your jib, they'd lumber into the air, fix you with their unintelligent eyes and swoop at your head till you were gone.

A 'cultural landscape' they called it, but up on the island's heights, giddied by the cloud shadows over the turf, and by sea and sky, and distracted everywhere by birds, you could be forgiven for asking where, in this wild place, was the culture? But soon I understood that, ranged along the clifftops, camouflaged by stone and turf, were yet more cleits. They were everywhere. The more you saw, clinging to steep slopes or perched on rocky tables, the more there were.

Perhaps it was his white beard, but when Ian strapped on the portable surveying equipment, he looked like a sort of techno-prophet. The hefty batteries were carried in a backpack with an aerial sticking out, and he held before him a tall staff with a saucer-sized satellite dish mounted on top. This also had a small monitor attached, called a data-logger, which he used to tap in figures and instructions and read off relevant numbers. Amongst other things, it told him how many satellites were present beyond the clouds at any given moment—they used those of the US-controlled NAVSTAR system—and how they were disported in the skies, and how many others would shortly rise over our horizon.

When Ian explained this to me, he used the language of stars, spoke about 'constellations' of satellites. He told me that to get a GPS reading you need at least four out of the twenty-four NAVSTAR satellites orbiting above you. With these in place, and with their readings fine-tuned by a small base station erected in the village, you could scramble all over the island, and pinpoint your position to the nearest centimetre.

A centimetre? I was appalled. Too much accuracy! It was like pinning a moth to a board.

But, Ian went on to say that, actually, such precise surveying reveals that nothing is truly fixed. For example, when the tide comes in on the west coast, the whole UK landmass dips a little under the colossal weight of water. Furthermore, the UK is creeping toward Norway, just a fraction, year by year. The surveyors' equipment can detect these infinitesimal shifts.

'And the cleits,' I asked. 'Do you know how many there are?'

'Mary Harman counted 1400 on Hirta alone, more on the other islands, and the stacks . . .'

'And you're going to survey every single one of them down to a centimetre's accuracy?'

The cliff heights didn't dizzy me, but that did.

So it began. Every structure the team approached over the next days received the same treatment. Ian, with the rover-receiver, consulted his screen and took an initial reading, calling out ten-figure coordinates for his colleague Adam to note down. Then he moved around the building, taking a new reading every few paces. By joining these dots, the building's 'footprint' appeared on his screen. Each was a oval with a gap at one end for the door, a shape like a broken link. Which they were, in a sense, now the people were gone, and the land supported no one.

Adam took notes the old-fashioned way, with pencil and paper. His job was to describe in natural language the building's state of repair, and any distinguishing features. 'This one's a side-loader,' he would say, meaning that, unusually, the door was on the longer wall. 'Aw, its hat's blown off!' meant the turf roof was gone. He noticed that those built on steep slopes had a vent at the lower end, presumably to let the draught through, to keep the contents dry. That the walls were thicker than the space they contained. Sam took photographs, so there would be a visual record, too.

It was patient work, which proceeded a few windblown yards at a time. They'd approach a new cleit, press the right buttons, take the GPS readings, measure, make notes, photograph, move on. Weathers and cloud shadows moved swiftly across the island, a sudden stinging hailstorm would arrive and pass on, and the sun would come out again. We always had to shout to be heard. Record, and move on. I thought the cleits curious, half nature and half culture, with their stone walls and turf roofs that shivered in the breeze. We could measure them all we liked, but they were still mysterious. Always we were in sight of the sea. Waves broke against rocks far below, sending out white spume and turquoise wash.

This careful recording was a wholly different way of looking at St Kilda to what I'd have done alone. Alone, I'd have rushed around, thrilled but hampered by a kind of illiteracy, unable to read the land. I wouldn't have studied the cats'-paw pattern of lichen on a lintel-stone, so similar to the patterns made by the wind on the surface of the sea below. I wouldn't have noticed a clump of tiny violets quivering on a cleit roof. Sheep liked to shelter in the cleits. Their interiors smelled of dung; sometimes a rotting carcass sent us away gagging.

Often we wondered exactly what a particular cleit had been used for. Especially when the surveyors, again led by the sure-footed Sam, had to edge two or three hundred feet down steep slopes, to reach cleits so far down they looked like turtles that had climbed up out of the sea. Surely these must have held eggs or birds the St Kildan men had taken, climbing barefoot with horse-hair ropes round their waists.

When such questions arose, it was strange there was no one to ask. You couldn't just nip down to the village and ask someone. As Sam had intimated the first night, it all seemed very recent and very ancient at once. Ancient, because all was stone. Recent, because the evacuation had been a media event, with reporters and cameras. Someone told us that that there was one St Kildan woman still alive, who had been a small child in 1930, and who was living her final days in a Hebridean care home.

———————

We had a run of good weather, and the teams worked long hours. They surveyed cleit after cleit, in friendly rivalry. A hundred a day! Not only cleits: occasionally a turf dyke, or something that may have once been an enclosure. If it could be interpreted as a man-made structure, it was surveyed.

There was method in it—the sequence they followed was Dr Harman's. She had taken photographs; our task meant matching her small black-and-white photographs taken thirty years ago with a real world-view of changing light and colour and tugging wind. It was my job to scout ahead. I'd seek salient features in the photo, a jagged lintel, say, or a stone shaped like a horse's head, and look for those. It was obvious from the photos that time was taking its toll. Every cleit looked more tired, more loose, was heading fractionally toward collapse.

'I know,' Jill said later. 'It's a pity, but this is what we're doing—studying how cleits die.'

Thus, when the surveyors moved over the island, from one feature to the next, conducting their short ritual, they were like priests, giving each of these little buildings the last rites.

Of course, you can only record what remains. What's gone is gone. Every rock, every feature, on the island had a name. We worked around Claigeann an Tigh Faire, the Skull of the Watching House; the Lovers' Rock; Cam Mar; Mullach Sgar; but who knows how many other names are now forgotten. Maybe each of the cleits once had a name, now lost, too.

They had to work quickly, but there was always time to admire a pair of golden plover, innocently parading their bright speckles, then go carefully for fear of trampling their nest, or shield our eyes to watch a midair dogfight between a bonxie and a screaming seagull. Lunches were a sandwich taken huddled out of the wind, and from time to time there was an enforced break, a 'spike'—a short while when too few satellites were available for readings to be made. A 'spike' was a chance to sit against a high rock, eat wine gums, and comment on the sea and clouds and the birds' dramas. To my mind, a 'spike' had a special feel. Not that the satellites could 'see' us, but nonetheless it was a chance to be unobserved, free for a while. We were very high, not quite a satellite view, but high enough to see patterns on the sea's surface, long trails of shining water like the marks left behind by an ice-skater. We watched gannets dive, and puffins, those stout little householders, at the doors of their burrows. Once, a whale arched from the water below, blew and rolled down again, a black sigh.

Being with the surveyors taught me to change my focus. It was like the difference between looking through a window pane and looking at it. Look through the window, and you'd see the sea, wildness, distance, isolation. Look at it, and you saw utility, food security, domestic management. We moved between the Stone Age and the Age of Satellites. What separated them? Only thirty years. A mere thirty years after the St Kildan people had finally given up, defeated by their isolation, Telstar was launched, and the world had satellite communications. Thirty years. A fulmar can live longer than that, if left in peace.

There was a spike. Sam and Ian and Adam and I sat side by side, backs against a sheltering rock and watching the sea and tumbling birds, and wind-driven clouds crossing the blue sky. From here you could see the so-called Western Isles ranged faintly on the eastern horizon. You could close your eyes, feel the sun on your skin, and fancy yourself far from the modern world with all its technology, were it not for Ian checking his data-logger to see if more satellites had climbed into the cultural landscape of the heavens.

In truth, I found this level of scrutiny a little unnerving. It was disquieting, to be aware all the time of satellites prowling unseen above the sky, while examining a landscape others had created and left behind. Nothing here escaped notice—not a bird, not a stone, certainly not a person. St Kilda, far from being an escape, the remotes that German couple sought, and I had myself thought I might find those years ago on my first trip, was instead a place of comment and note. More than once I'd marvelled at the sheer number of cleits. Cleit-building seemed an absolute mania. After a week I began to wonder if they'd had an unstated purpose; if people had built small dark closets just to get some seclusion, some corrective to the sky, the sea and wind and each other.

Nothing escaped attention. One day a snowy owl wafted in over the sea, probably from Iceland. It wasn't long, of course, before he was spotted, and the news was relayed to us via the little VHF radios the surveyors carried in their pockets. The owl frequented a particular rocky overhang which gave him a view of the valley called Glen Mor, and once you knew where to look you could see him half a mile away, like a white-robed hermit at the door of a shrine.

Everyone knew the weather had to break, so the surveyors pressed on while they could. At five or six o'clock, depending on progress, Ian would get on the radio to the other team, and suggest calling it a day. Work was still work—we were glad to knock off. When we all met up, there were always snippets of news and details to exchange. To save lugging it up and down the hill every day, the roving receivers were stored overnight in a particularly strong cleit. I liked to see them being loaded through the dark entranceway. For a short while the cleit was brought back into use. It became a store again, a strong room, but for items its builders never dreamed of.

So were the working days. Amassing cleitfuls of data, recording against loss.

Cresting the hill homeward we could see at once if any new boats were anchored below. I always looked for Donald's yacht, but didn't see it. No doubt he was showing his clients other wonderful places.

Down in the village, too, there was news to catch up on, the events that we'd missed. If winds were favourable the place was in constant activity. One morning, a cruise liner put in, landing 200 visitors for the warden to cope with. One visitor had been so overcome with emotion or agoraphobia that the nurse stationed at the radar base had to be called to coax her back to her boat. Another day, a helicopter carrying a Japanese film crew had flown illegally close to the cliffs, panicking the birds, which are supposed to be pro-tected. The helicopter was traced by its number—nothing goes unnoticed—and there were furious phone calls. A couple of days after that, an environmental health officer arrived, courtesy of the base helicopter, to do his rounds.

You soon get into the swing of life at Village Bay, but in truth I didn't care for the place. Not because it was sullied by the base and its Cold War paranoia; not because it wasn't 'remote' enough—though with the satellites and cruise liners and environmental health officers, you do wonder what 'remote' might mean. It was the village itself that troubled me, those cottages we walked past twice a day en route to plot and measure every last jot their people had left behind. They didn't sing of a lost idyll, those cold empty doors. If the cottages spoke at all, it was to say—Look, they made their decision. They quit. They moved on.

For several days in a row we ladies in our boudoir were puz-zled by a persistent early-morning tap-tap-tapping at the window, until we discovered it was a pied wagtail, infuri-ated by his own reflection. Then, one morning, the sound changed. There was no pecking; instead the wind banged at the same east-facing, sea-facing window. A higher swell licked along the rocks; overnight, clouds had covered the hills. The village was as I'd seen it the first time, fleetingly. '*Nach du bha'n a Hirst!*' The forecast was for more wind, out of the dreaded east.

With the wind, there arose a dilemma. The skipper who'd brought us arrived with some day-trippers, and said he had space to take two or three of us back to Harris almost at once, if we wanted. To accept would mean leaving St Kilda a couple of days earlier than planned. But the forecast was such, the skipper warned, that it might be a full week before he was back.

For an hour I wandered round the village, swithering. Stay, or go? Leave St Kilda?

In the little museum were the nineteenth-century photographs. People with weather-worn faces in homespun clothes. Go or stay? I was hardly the first to have faced that choice. There came to mind that poor German couple on the yacht, who had so dreamed of coming to St Kilda. To leave early did seem a terrible luxury. But, then again, my children were still young; another week would be too long.

The power station droned, soft rain fell, ewes and their lambs sheltered in the doors of cleits. Ach. Enough. I went to get ready. It wasn't as if I had work to do, like the surveyors. To linger on St Kilda just for the sake of it would merely have been romance.

LA CUEVA

———

THE WALLS OF THE CHAMBER are the colour of old ivory, but damp, amphibian, as though they still remember the long-ago rivers which formed them. They bulge toward us, gravid, then shrink into shadow.

One of the two girls carries a lamp; her friend is too encumbered with a large leather handbag. The girls are student age. When the girls arrived laughing at the guide's desk, in the cool of the cave mouth the bag had made me smile. Funny thing to bring into a cave. Now we are two or three chambers in, the air is weighty and humid; it smells of iron and deep earth. The way we have come from is in darkness. So is the way ahead. We move through passages in a clot of light, cast by the two hissing paraffin lamps. When the lamps move, shadows lope along the walls.

Now we are gathered around him, the guide is speaking quietly. A lean young man, he's a member of the family who rediscovered the caves a hundred years ago. I can pick up certain words: *agua*, water, *murcielagos*, bats—a cluster of whom, like a scrunch of black pubic hair, hang from the roof above. Tomas says there are thousands more bats, asleep in further, deeper galleries. He says that's how the caves were discovered—by bats. Two farmers, his own forebears, had been looking for bat guano to fertilise their olive trees, so they took care at dawn to watch where the bats went, and, like the Pied Piper, the bats led them to an opening in the mountainside. So the dance began again, animals and humans and cave.

Now we're looking at stalagmites, by the soft lamplight. Some are seven or eight feet high, clotted, fatty shades, but hard and damp. They're like huge pathological specimens, the kind preserved in jars in anatomy museums, leached of colour. Perhaps that's what gives the cave its solemnity: it feels like we're doing something intimate, transgressive, which we can speak about only in whispers. We have entered a body, and are moving through its ducts and channels and sites of processes. The very chamber we stand in is streaked with iron-red; it's like the inside of a cranium, a mind-space, as though the cave were thinking us.

'El Castillo—you see,' says Tomas, lifting his lamp. 'This one is like a castle! And this one'—a figure drenched in calcium carbonate—'like a bride's dress. And look—we call this one The Family, you see—four people, two big, two small.' Smiling, we take up the game. It's reassuring, in this gallery of uncanny forms, to map them onto things we know in the world outside. 'That one up there—like an owl!' 'Ugh—see—a guillotine.' 'Like' is the word. This is like that, connected.

We are deep in a hall of similes.

Leaving the stalagmites, we climb a stone ramp in which steps have been cut, and enter into another stone space, higher and wider. The cave mouth, the outside world, is already a memory. This time the lamps reveal a high ceiling with formations like the gills on the underside of mushrooms. The air is steady and humid. When the five of us are gathered round, Tomas steps toward the wall with his lamp, to show us a thick, black stain on the pale wall, which begins at the floor and tapers up into the gloom of the roof space. *Fuego*, he says—fire. For thousands of years, Palaeolithic hunter-gatherers crept in here to sleep, bands of twenty or twenty-five people. So long ago, the soot has calcified, has turned to stone.

A soot stain on a cave wall. It makes my neck creep. It's like gazing back to the birth of human consciousness.

The girl beside me shifts the weight of her bag. I shouldn't have smiled. Stone tools, water, berries, wood to burn. Her baby. Wherever she went, she'd have been encumbered.

The lamps move, the shadows spin, we're moving on. But first, just as we are about to file into a narrow passage out of the fire-hall, Tomas stops. He wants us to understand something about the space we're leaving and the deeper space we'll shortly enter. A distinction. This place with the fire, he says, was for everyone, communal, together. It had been used for thousands of years. Frightening maybe, to crawl in here by tallow-lamp, past the stalagmites, up the stone ramp, but better to be in here, all together, than out in the night with its weathers and beasts. However, the deeper caves we are about to enter may only have been used by specialists, and not for ordinary purposes. He says—do you understand? We think it was for ritual, and not for everyone.

We have entered a place, this cave-body, full of similes and transformations, where a stalagmite becomes a castle, fire turns to stone—but also a place of distinctions. We nod gravely as Tomas speaks. When we distinguish and segregate, we are serious-minded. When we make connections, when we say look, this is like a dress, like an owl, I am like you—then we laugh.

We leave the chamber with the smoke stain. The two men enter the passage first. They have to duck and turn their shoulders sideways, the gap is so narrow. The girl with the bag is ahead of me; her friend with the lamp comes behind. I can smell the lamp, hissing like an animal, its body heat at my calf.

———————

There was a time—until very recently in the scheme of things—when there were no wild animals, because every animal was wild; and humans were few. Animals, and animal presence over us and around us. Over every horizon, animals. Their skins clothing our skins, their fats in our lamps, their bladders to carry water, meat when we could get it.

Now we're crouching, like hunters, because Tomas, who is also crouching, has angled his lamp to throw the soft light into the back of a low niche, and when we look, we gasp, because in the back of the niche is a horse. So fresh! Part of a horse: with a single red line the artist has caught the droop of the jaw; another line is its neck. A rub of mane, small forward-pointing ears and a mere gesture where the left leg joins the body is enough to show that the horse is walking. That's all—the forequarters of a small wild horse, walking in an unseen landscape.

We don't linger; too much light will cause the paint to fade. Tomas moves on, the horse returns to its long darkness. But soon two male ibex appear on the walls, or through the walls, with long spines and elegant back-tilted horns. They're side by side, facing right and tilted upward, as though cautiously moving uphill and away. Then, two small bulls are revealed to us. One bull is drifting slowly upwards, his horned head melded into that of another bull, angled down. No animal is complete; all are partial, half-disclosed, which is much how we encounter them alive.

Here and there a dark smudge on the wall still shows where an artist's lamp rested, smoking a little, while he or she worked. The very paints are cave minerals mixed with animal fat. But why the animals should appear in deep caves, we don't know. Hallucinations, maybe. Shaman work. Perhaps people were drawing, in the other sense. Coaxing animal presence out of the deep source, the cave-uterus.

We are deep in metaphor, the membranes between body and stone, and cave and animal are dissolved: melded, like the two turning bulls. We move on. Every time I think, surely, this is the end, we move on.

There is nothing to betray the presence of water until a drop falls and silent ripples spread at our feet. The water is perfectly clear, the floor under the water visible as thick grey silt. In that silt, Tomas says, was discovered much Neolithic pottery.

Again he lifts his lamp. Behind the pool the cave wall is a panel of crazed black hatchings and scores, like combs or rakes. Tomas says—'these are Neolithic, made maybe 5000 years ago. By then the people were farmers, no longer hunter-gatherers. Everyone tries to interpret these marks. Many people say they are calendars but no one knows.'

Whatever they were, compared to the Palaeolithic animals, these black hatches seem anxious and nervy, as though they addressed new human concerns. To what problems were such markings the solution? The Neolithic traces leave you with that tip-of-the-tongue feeling, like you know what they are, just can't quite bring it to mind. But the red horse and the ibex and the floating bulls, so much, much older— those we recognise at once.

'You see,' Tomas says. 'They knew there was water here.' They must have told the children, even brought them all the way down here, saying—remember this cave, in case the springs run dry in the world above. Take a lamp, hold your nerve, keep going and don't give up, there *will* be water.

The wall is close, the floor uneven. When I put out a hand to steady myself, I'm very aware of that touch, aware of our exhaled breath. Many other caves which hold Palaeolithic art—Chauvet, for example—are closed to lay visitors. At the dramatic (and younger) Lascaux, with its teeming bestiary, one visits a replica, fabricated above ground. These places are closed to preserve them. As long ago, specialists and researchers only may enter, but not ordinary folk.

You wonder if this is what drives us, what has brought us thus far: discriminations and resentments on the one hand. You, but not you. On the other hand, our ability, born perhaps of thousands of years of watching the transforming play of firelight—to think in simile, in metaphor. We can say look, that shadow is like an antler, this line suggests an ibex horn, that girl is a deer, this problem is like that; therefore, that solution might just do the trick. The connective leaps, the careful taxonomies, how our minds work.

We leave the pool. In the midst of the Neolithic panel of hash marks and scores, there is a bird-man, flying with outstretched wings.

There must have been a day when people quit the cave for the last time. A gradual withdrawing, then an age of forgetting. Perhaps there have been several such times of darkness, when only animals entered to shelter, then periods of rediscovery, when the cave fulfilled new needs.

Different needs for different eras. Our Palaeolithic kinship with animals, with nature, is over, broken, or so we say. Strange, though, that it should have been animals—bats—who led the way to the cave this time round. And that it should have happened just as we were discovering a new relationship, closer than ever: discovering that we'd all travelled together, separating and overlapping, out of a deep, shared evolutionary origin.

The lamps shift again. The shadows lope. Incredibly, we are going on, farther still.

MAGPIE MOTH

———

THE LOCHAN, one of the numberless lochans on the moor, was kidney-shaped, and the breeze had formed ripples at its eastern end. It held no reeds or water lilies; it was just a blank pool formed in a complex bit of land.

I was eating breakfast by its side, and in due course I made my way down to the water to rinse the bowl. There were three large rocks in the water, big enough to crouch on. The residue of the milk swilled away; I dabbled the spoon.

Then I saw a moth. It caught my eye, because it was floating captive in the triangle of water held between the three rocks. An attractive moth, its white wings patterned with brown and orangey dabs. It was pinned down, without the pin, held flat by the surface tensions of the water.

Maybe I should just have left it be—why intervene, after all? It only leads to trouble, but I was crouched above a stricken moth with a spoon in my hand. Deliverance, in the middle of nowhere, in the form of the Great Teaspoon. What were the chances of that?

As soon as the spoon took up the moth's infinitesimal weight, the creature jerked its legs, but it was so water-logged that its wings clamped to the spoon and wrapped around the spoon's rim onto its convex side. I didn't fancy scraping its wings with my fingernail, so lowered the spoon back into the water. The moth floated free and relaxed into its shape of open helplessness. This time I lifted the spoon more carefully, trying to ensure the moth was centred in the spoon's concavity. The trick, I reckoned, was to bring a little water, too, enough to slide the moth from the spoon onto the rock the right way up.

Partial success. The moth lay on the rock. The wings on the left were unfurled, but those on the right were all scrunched up. The rocks were covered in thin dabs of yeasty lichens, and against those colours the moth, so open and flagrant on the water, was immediately lost.

Though the morning sun was warm enough to dry the moth's wings, I doubted now they would function; some sort of coating, their back-of-the-cupboard mothy dusti-ness, looked like it had been ruined. Besides, there was something about the balance of the moth which was awry.

Awry, but it was moving. With some apprehension, I looked more closely. With one antenna the moth was testing the minute facets of rock, a back-and-forth movement like a blind man's stick. But something was certainly lopsided, and I didn't like it. Perhaps I should just have left it alone. A fish would have got it soon enough.

Then I remembered my magnifying glass. It had been my birthday, and a friend had given me a foldaway magnifying glass. The moth, having been rescued for good or ill, would now suffer itself to be scrutinised. But not without dread: I feared I'd done it damage. I was in there, implicated now.

The glass showed me its two black lightless moth eyes, and a tuft of fur at the back of its head. There was the rolled spotted rag of its body, not three quarters of an inch long. A magpie moth. Why magpie? There was nothing pied about it. Moth eyes. What do they see with their moth eyes?

But now, as I angled the glass, the cause of its lopsidedness became apparent. The tip of the moth's left front leg was hooked round and glued to its left eye by a tiny droplet of water. A water-drop—what strength is there in that? Too much for a moth to break, apparently. It was stuck in a grotesque posture, but also a bit comic: it looked like a gentleman holding up a monocle, the better to inspect me, as I peered at it through my own lens.

The monocled moth. The loop formed by the bent leg would accept something very small. A reed, perhaps, but there were none. The nib of a pen. Half lying on the rock, magnifying glass in one hand, I fumbled to open the pen in my pocket. Then, with the moth's black eye in my sights, I made one tiny tweak; the moth's leg was free.

Like one released from a spell, the moth began a frantic crawling over the rock. God, I thought, it's in pain. I've wounded it. With its good wings open, as pretty as ever, the right wings still furled up, the moth dragged itself over the rock-edge and walked headfirst down the sheer side, straight back toward the water. A few inches down, however, it stopped. It was in the shade, all four legs like guy ropes, holding it to the rock. An instinct, maybe, to get out of the sight of birds.

Enough. The bubble of my attention popped. I stood too quickly, swooned a little, because there was the wide moor, the loch and breezy grasses reaching for miles, all scaling up to meet me. I'd been absorbed in the minuscule: a moth's eye, a dab of lichen; been granted a glimpse into the countless millions of tiny processes and events that form the moor. Millions! Tiny creatures, flowers, bacteria, opening, growing, dividing, creeping about their business. It's all happening out there, and all you have to do, girl, is get your foot out of your eye.

Ach, perhaps I should have left the moth alone; I'd probably done it more harm than good. After all, laid on the water, its patterned wings unfolded and perfect, it looked to be in a state of bliss, but what do we know?

I shook myself, went back up to the car.

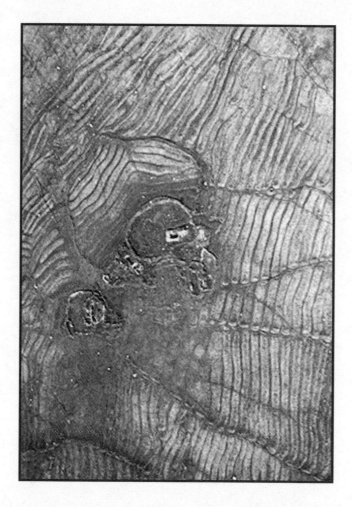

ON RONA

FAR OVER THE HORIZON, out in the north Atlantic, where one might expect a clear run to Iceland or even Labrador, or, if anything, just a guano-streaked gull-slum, the island of Rona is one last green hill rising from the waves.

Or so they tell me. It's forty miles out, several hours' sailing, but pretty soon I was prostrate on the aft deck, shivering under the wind- and engine-noise. From deep in my sick cocoon I heard the others calling they could see Rona on the horizon, then more cold, salt-immobiled ages passed until the boat slowed, the wind-rush dropped. When they cut the engines and sent down the anchor, I felt gratitude, but then the boat began wallowing. Worse than the leaping waves was that awful wallowing. There were guillemots, but they sounded as though they were stuck down a well, because we were in the shelter of a geo—a steep-sided inlet. There were dark cliffs on either side, a rattling as the dinghy was lowered, and voices, one, a man's, saying, 'Let's get her ashore.'

I must have jumped from the dinghy and scrambled up the slabby rocks as per instructions and, meeting grass, collapsed on it. A green unheaving bosom. Blessed deep core of steady rock, reaching down and down. Lay there till the nausea passed, and the shivering.

Coming back to myself, I heard land-birds, starlings, rolled over, looked up at the sky, smelled a sweet smell, some kind of wildflower, thrift maybe. How lush the grass was! That surprised me. Lush-long and harsh at once. The sky was high and bright with fleet clouds. Lay there, as slowly the sun and breeze dried my waterproofs. Bob the skipper blew the boat's horn as he left, then Stuart and Jill appeared up from the shore, grinning, laden with gear, and we were on our own.

So, for a short while last summer we had Rona to ourselves. Alone in the encircling ocean, me and my companions, Stuart Murray and Jill Harden. Stuart's of that sterling tradition of self-taught naturalists; a bird-man who says, 'Believe what you see'—but a prerequisite of that believing is a great accuracy of seeing, and a rough idea of what you're looking at. For him Rona was an old and beloved haunt; he had brought notes in his own hand from thirty years before—lists and columns of figures pertaining to puffin colonies, to black back gulls and storm petrels. Jill is an archaeologist and, like Stuart, not one to be fanciful. Though she knew most of the Scottish islands, Rona was new to her; it intrigued her because, despite being so remote, as we would say nowadays, when our sense of centre is different, it had been inhabited for centuries. On its south-facing side, there's a long-abandoned village surrounded by

a swirl of field systems, and a very early Christian chapel.
These remains are themselves ancient, but who knows what
lies beneath.

Those two, Jill and Stuart, were great observers. Late on
the afternoon we arrived, when I'd recovered myself and
we'd unpacked all the food and gear, I was out walking,
when I caught sight of Stuart in characteristic pose. He
was hunkered against an exposed rock that offered views
of a cliff loud with guillemots and kittiwakes. He had binoculars in one hand and a notebook pressed open on his
knee. I was back at the bothy when he arrived through the
heavy door.

'Well?' I said, meaning, 'How goes the world?'

'No' bad.'

'What were you doing?'

'Just having a damn good look.'

'And?'

'Kittiwakes have young, two sometimes.'

'That's good.'

'It *is* good. Maybe it's the start of a recovery. How many
gulls have you seen?'

'Me?' I said. 'Gulls? Some. A few.'

A few standing on a broken wall, keeping a steely eye on
us interlopers.

'Exactly. There were near a thousand pairs of great black
backs in 2001, chicks running everywhere. They've completely collapsed.'

Then Jill arrived back, too, carrying her drawing board.
Already she'd been down at the chapel, and the semi-
subterranean village where she'd spend much of her time,

brushing earth from stones with her strong hands, crawling into passages, shining a torch into gaps unlit for ages.

'Well?' I said again.

That merry smile. 'Ooh, interesting.'

'What were you doing?'

'Oh, just . . . having a look!'

Inhabited once, but now the island is returned to birds and seals; grey seals in thousands breed there, many seemingly disinclined to leave. Every day, all around the shore, were rocks softened by the shapes of seals, watching us from the waters. What we called 'the bothy' was properly a field station for a team of biologists who arrive every November to study the seals at pupping time. The bothy was a green shed, galeproof and insulated, with two rooms, one with bunks and the other with a kitchen and table, and a container for well-water. Every store and roof-space was crammed with equipment and supplies. There were spades and ropes and cupboards of tinned food, and a shelf of fantasy novels and thrillers, which says much about Rona in November. There was even a handwritten copy of Kipling's 'If', pinned to the wall—'If you can keep your head when all about you / are losing theirs'. But there was little fear of that: though we were on our own and far from anywhere, Stuart and Jill were both relaxed and robust, old hands at this kind of thing.

That first night seasickness and sea air had done for me; come twilight, I dozed in my bunk a couple of hours, but when Jill came and said they were going to the village, I got up again and, like the others, made ready to go out. It was nearly midnight, and we went out, because, well, how often do you get the chance to ramble round an uninhabited island, in the northern ocean, in summer? But also, there was something in particular we wanted to witness, which happened only in the darkest hours. Saturday night, and we had a date in town—but instead of glad rags we pulled on winter waterproofs and hats, because even in July the sea winds were persistent and cold.

———————

The island is only a mile and half long. It has one fertile hill, and two flat near-barren peninsulas, one pointing north, one southwest, like two mismatching wings. There are no beaches, all is cliff, swooping now high, now low, and cut with many geos. The sea prowled into every geo; by night its sound seemed muted, though now and then the breeze brought whoops of seal-song. Clouds were gathering, but that was good, Stuart said: the darker, the better.

We walked westward up a slight rise, which at its crest gave views down a long slope to the ragged peninsula called Sceapull, which soon surrendered to the waves. A dusty, antique sort of light lay over the island; the sea was the colour of tarnished silver. The path led across a hillside, then through a gap in an earthen dyke. At once, within the dyke, the land began to rise and fall in ridges, like those of a vast scallop shell, waist-high ridges between shadow-filled troughs, all with a pelt of long grass that shivered in the wind. The ridges curved downhill toward the sea. Hundreds of years ago oats or barley would have been raised on them, but now, long overgrown, they had become sculptural, land art.

We passed through that strange estate, then arrived at the shell of St Ronan's chapel. Just four stone walls, all speckled with lichen, a low doorway, no roof at all. It faced the southern sea, and between the chapel and the cliffs a quarter-mile away were ovals and pockets of darkness, half dug into the earth, and bound by overgrown turf walls—all that remained of the village. Beyond that, beat of the waves.

This was what we'd come for, something faraway and special, so we settled ourselves against the chapel wall to wait.

I think I fell asleep. Half asleep, but started awake because someone had laughed right in my ear. It came again—a stuttery laugh in the air, a burst of high chatter, sudden as a match-strike. At once it was answered from within the wall itself. A shape tilted fast overhead and Jill beside me said, 'Look, that's one—they're coming.' Even as she spoke, another spat of glee came, conjured out of the night air; now several dark shapes were darting about the chapel walls, quick like bats but not bats. They chattered as they flew, and from deep within the walls came rapid replies. Jill cast me a laughing look, as more birds appeared from nowhere to chase and chatter around us, so close we could feel the thrum of their wings on our hair.

You have to go a long way to find a breeding colony of Leach's fork-tailed petrels; to a handful of the farthermost islands, St Kilda, the Flannans, and here, Rona, where on summer nights they make the quick dash ashore. Mate calls to mate, *dit-dit diddle-dit*!, rival pursues rival, one partner creeps back into his burrow-nest, allowing the other to be off on her small black wings, far out to sea.

The call, to our human ears, sounded like laughter. At the darkest hour, the walls, like a hive, were busy with birds. They're small as swifts, but their challenge isn't the ocean storms, it's the short race ashore. Great skuas—bonxies—prey on them, god knows how, hence their dash by moonlight—except, they prefer no moon. They prefer the darkest of summer nights.

Surf, and seal-song, and petrel glee. By about two o'clock, dawn was breathing onto the northeast sky again, and there was an urgent wartime feel in the air, of subterfuge and thrill, and exchanges of the birds' high, rapid Morse.

Stuart had been prowling about the village; now he came back, a white-haired figure rounding the chapel end.

'It's wonderful!' I whispered.

We stood in the chapel doorway, as dark bird-shapes chased above its ancient walls.

'How far out do they go?'

'Right to the edge of the continental shelf.'

'How far's that?'

'We're about halfway there. Another fifty miles.'

The birds jinked about our heads as we spoke; if they saw or heard us at all, they paid no heed.

'Just *magic*!'

'There's no' many . . .'

'There's loads, look . . .'

But he shook his head. 'No, there's no'.'

———————

Leach's petrels are rare, so under European law we're supposed to keep a weather eye on them. This was Stuart's task—he'd come to Rona to count their secret nests. He had done the same ten years ago; over the next days he'd do it again.

In the morning—though the sun had been high for hours—we again made our way through the fields-systems to the village. The ruins were all innocence by light of day; not a sound came from them, nor from the stones of the chapel. Human presence and retreat was all they admitted to; they denied all knowledge of the night's merriment.

We were blessed with the weather. I had the sensation I always have on Atlantic islands, in summertime, when the clouds pass quickly and light glints on the sea—a sense that the world is bringing itself into being moment by moment. Arising and passing away in the same breath. Stuart, however, meant business. From a rucksack he produced some bamboo canes and plastic tags. Then he handed me a Sony Walkman.

'Right,' he said. 'Give three blasts, about thirty seconds, then move on.'

'Where?'

'Anywhere that looks likely.'

Looks likely. We were standing by a curved waist-high wall that contained an oval space now brightly carpeted with silverweed. Two stones jutted up from the wall-head like praying hands.

'Does that look likely?'

He shrugged. 'Try it.'

I held the Walkman to a tiny gap between stone and turf, and pressed the button. The tape whirred, then issued the *dit-dit diddly-dit* of a Leach's petrel, and at once, from under the stones, a muffled but outraged householder *dit diddle-ditted* right back again. It made me laugh, but Stuart wrote a figure on a plastic marker and rammed it into the turf.

'You do the rest of these walls. This'll be your patch. We'll do the village every day. Jill's taking the graveyard. I'll do the chapel dyke.'

'Does it work if you play them Abba?' I asked, but he just gave me a long look.

It was a joy. In sunshine and a businesslike breeze, I made my way around the old walls, pausing every few yards to press the button and quickly learning the 'likely places'. Some burrows were neat round holes in the turf; the birds dig them out with their feet. If I saw such a burrow, I played the tape, then pressed my ear to the turf. Silence was disappointing, but every time a bird responded from within, it made me laugh again. If a burrow was live, if a bird was tucked inside, there were tiny signs: broken grass stalks, a discreet dropping. You could sometimes smell their peculiar rich, musty odour. Some burrows had no visible door; the response came from deep within green tussocks, as if from a fairy boudoir. Now and again the tape elicited some sexy Eartha Kitt purring—that was the female. Only males made the chatterbox call; sometimes if one piped up, he set off his neighbours, too, so a turf wall, centuries old, warming in the sun, started up like a barrel organ.

I found myself saying, 'Thank you' and 'Sorry', and began to feel like a door-to-door salesman, except, if I looked behind me, there was the ocean, brightly shifting everywhere, meeting the sky in every shade of grey. A little farther uphill, around the chapel, Jill and Stuart worked at

their own sections, leaning in to their own walls, as if listening to the heartbeats of stones.

But when we met to compare notes Stuart was again
muttering darkly. It was not good, he said. Not like last
time. Worrying.

Over the next ten days, he covered the entire island, from
the lighthouse at the eastern clifftop down to the ends
of both storm-scoured peninsulas. Sometimes Jill and I
helped. We laid blue nylon ropes over the ground to mark
off strips of land, so we could tell where we'd been when
every stone began to look like every other. Within the roped
sections, we crawled a few yards apart, playing our tapes
under rocks and cairns. Sometimes birds answered, and soon
I couldn't see an unexplored rock without my heart giving
a little leap—a likely place! We found bits of birds, a cradle
of seals' ribs, the exquisite skeleton of a starfish, no bigger
than a thumbnail. It was a curious task, very intimate, to
sail to a faraway island, then crawl over it on hands and
knees, like pilgrims or penitents.

Every morning we worked the village, which held by far
the greatest concentration of birds, and soon developed a
feel for the colony's dynamic. If a bird who'd replied every
day for three days was suddenly absent, he got a cross against
his number in my notebook, and I knew that he'd slipped
out to sea in the small hours. Gone from the chapel, from
the village. A wing and a prayer. Now his mate would be
sitting meekly on her single egg, a dark eye in the darkness
within the dyke.

While Stuart spoke to the birds, Jill communed with stones. First she concentrated on St Ronan's chapel. It's just a shell now, the stones of its western gable much collapsed. It stands at the southern wall of an enclosure, and within the enclosure is a little graveyard, very old. The turf has risen over the centuries, so the humble gravestones, hewn of the sparkly island feldspar, tilt this way and that like little sinking ships.

Nothing is known of St Ronan but his name, which, oddly, means 'little seal'—as if he'd been a Rona selkie who'd swapped his sealskin for the habit of a monk. Doubtless he was one of the early Scots-Irish monks, who sailed from his monastery to seek 'a desert place in the sea', where he could live a life of austerity and prayer. Hundreds of years later, the people built the chapel in his name, and buried their dead beside it. Now those people are gone, too, and their graveyard is a poignant place.

But suddenly it was en fête. This was Jill's doing. One day she went around the graveyard and festooned it with little orange flags on wires, one beside every stone, and the flags snapped in the breeze, so the cemetery seemed to be celebrating a day of the dead. She was plotting the grave-markers on a chart; the orange flags helped her see them as she measured their distance from a baseline: a measuring tape strung across the enclosure wall to wall. She was doing this because the stones were going missing. By studying black-and-white photographs from the 1930s or 1950s, she could tell that the stone crosses were being quietly stolen away—and, by dint of wind and weather, the medieval chapel was ever more collapsed. It troubled her. The chapel, village and all the surrounding fields are a Scheduled Ancient Monument, in the care of the state, but the state is far away and has more pressing concerns. So Jill said, 'We can at least plot them, so there's a record of what there was.' Really, she'd like to get people out here, experts from official agencies, an architect, or a drystone dyker, who could do some discreet shoring up and save the chapel from complete ruination.

One bright afternoon I held measuring poles and called out the numbers she needed, while Jill, a black baseball cap pulled over her thick hair, bent over a board and mapped the people's graves.

Of course it made us think of them. The long-dead people whose graves we knelt on. We called them 'them' and spoke about them every day. How did they live, what were their lives like, these people who'd managed for generations, out here alone in the sea?

The Rona people weren't unique; they were Gaels, part of the wider culture of the Western Isles, and, as Jill kept reminding us, the sea then was a conduit not a barrier. Nonetheless they lived a long way from any neighbours, had to fend for themselves, with their fields and few cattle and seabirds' eggs. But by the time Martin Martin wrote his travel journal of the Western Isles, in 1695, the people were already gone. 'That ancient race,' he called them, 'perfectly ignorant of most of those vices that abound in the world'— and when you wander round their village and look out at the uninterrupted sea, you know why.

Ronan's name is known, but the names of those buried under the turf are lost, save for one tantalising detail, which Martin provides: the Rona people, he says 'took their surname from the colour of the sky, rainbow and clouds'.

'Such work,' Jill would say, as we strolled through the overgrown fields. When I asked her who had first come to Rona, if it were Neolithic or Bronze Age people or what, she just smiled and said, 'Ooh, we don't know, do we?' The sea may have been the highway then, but it was still a long way to venture in a skin-covered boat.

The work, indeed. All those acres of undulating fields, built up by hand of the scant earth and seaweed. Outwith the enclosing dyke lay the rest of the island, which the people must have known down to every blade of grass, every stone. They must have felt acutely the turning of the seasons, the need to lay down stores and supplies, because summer was brief. We arrived in early July, when bog cotton was in bloom, soft white tufts facing into the wind. Two weeks later, its seeds clung to rocks and grasses, or were out to sea and lost.

Daily, our sense of time slowed, days expanded like a wing. The days were long in the best, high-summer sense; at night we put up storm shutters on the bothy window to make it dark enough to sleep. Time was clouds passing, a sudden squall, a shift in the wind. Often we wondered what it would do to your mind if you were born here, and lived your whole life within this small compass. To be named for the sky or the rainbow, and live in constant sight and sound of the sea. After a mere fortnight I felt lighter inside, as though my bones were turning to flutes.

St. Ronan rode to Rona on the back of a seamonster, so the legend says. Monster or boat, he'd have jumped ashore giving prayers of thanks, sometime in the eighth century.

Whether he was really alone, as romanticists would have it, or whether others came with him—monks, lay penitents, men without women—well, as Jill would say, we don't know, do we? Surely it would have taken more than one to do the spadework; even saints must eat. And if there were people on Rona already, people who knew exactly how many souls the island would support, watching as the Christians' boat drew nearer—we don't know that, either.

But we know what the saint sought, because on faraway Rona there survives something unique. A tiny building. To enter, you must first enter the chapel. Then, low on the eastern gable is another doorway, just a square of darkness with a lintel of white quartz, as though it were Neolithic. You have to crawl, but once inside you can stand freely. At first it seems wholly dark, and it smells of damp earth, but as your eyes adjust, stars of daylight begin to spangle here and there overhead, where, over the many centuries, the stones have slipped a little—so after a while it's like being in a wild planetarium.

Darkness, earth—and a sudden quiet; no wind or surf— you find yourself in a place from which all the distracting world is banned. Then you see the stonework. The little oratory is beautifully made, and has stood for 1200 years. A low stone altar stands against the east wall. So there is one thing we know of the saint—he had a feel for stone; strong hands. Or someone did. Having sailed here and claimed this island of sea-light and sky and seals and crying birds, he built himself a world-denying cell.

Two or three times, when Stuart was inquiring of the birds, and Jill of stones, I crept into the oratory, and waited till my eyes adjusted to the low light. I went warily, because a fulmar had made her nest in a corner; too close and she'd spit. A fulmar guarded the saint's cell, and it was strange to think there were Leach's petrels secreted in the walls. Sea-birds, named for St Peter, who walked on water, had colonised a cell built by a saint named for a seal.

I crept in just to wonder what he did in there, Ronan; to imagine him right there, in front of the altar, wrapped in darkness, rapt in prayer, closed off from the sensory world, the better to connect with . . . what?

I say we had the island to ourselves, but of course that's nonsense. There were the seals, and thousands of puffins, and colonies of terns on the low rocks, forever rising against some fresh outrage, and down among the rockpools, shags' slatternly nests.

One evening six swifts appeared, circled above the bothy and then vanished again. A party of Risso's dolphins arrived out of the blue, spent half an hour feeding just off the south side, then they, too, went on their way. The time of thrift had passed; every day, we met a flock of crossbills, of all things, which twittered round the island, feeding on thrift seeds. Crossbills are birds of the northern pine forest, but nary a pine tree here, and long sea miles to travel before they saw one again. There were about a hundred—the males were bright red, and the females brown, so when they all flew by they were like embers blown from a bonfire.

And, although no inhabited land was in sight, we weren't even truly alone in the ocean. Ten miles west, like the moon to Rona's fertile earth, rose the barren rock of Sula Sgeir—a gannet factory. And there was always the sense of the 'ancient race'. Personally, if ever I felt remote or cut off, it wasn't from the mainland far over the horizon, but from the abandoned village a quarter-mile away. There was something homely and recognisable about the oval shapes they made in the earth, and the humble chapel. We ate packet soups and tinned fruit, and looked out through the window at the relics of a lost intelligence, the long-forsaken fields, gilded in evening light.

———————

One morning, when the day was already established, I was washing my hair in a basin round at the bothy gable when I heard Stuart shouting. He'd gone out early, over to the north side, but here he was again, bawling from the hill crest and pointing out to sea. The wind had veered a little during the night, the sea was calm with a few white caps, and nothing seemed untoward, except—I grabbed a towel—for a party of gannets, ten or a dozen, a half-mile out from the island, which were quickly heading toward us. The birds' wings were a slow white flicker in the sunshine, as I thought later, like the flashes of paparazzi cameras. That's what I noticed first: that the gannets were flying in a peculiar way, limp and floppy, and in a bunch low above the water, not like the arrow-lines they usually form.

This all happened very quickly—the shout, the towel, the wide sea and floppy gannets. I'd seen gannets behave like that just once before, but once was enough; I yelled back, telling Stuart that we were onto it and, wiping soapy water from my eyes, barged into the bothy to find Jill.

We all arrived breathless at the cliffy rim of an inlet called Poll Thothatom. It was where we'd landed, steep-sided but for one obliging slope where you could jump ashore without fear of breaking your neck. Now, though, at the mouth of the inlet, with the wide sea behind them, five black fins pierced the water's surface.

Killer whales. The fins were glossy; one was tall and straight, a male's amid four smaller and more curved. The gannets had peeled away, and the killer whales were turning slowly around one another. Now and then an area of back surfaced, lay for a moment like an atoll, as the animal blew softly. It was as if, having arrived, they were taking time to agree strategy.

We stood side by side on the clifftop, watching with our hearts in our mouths. One thing we knew—they probably weren't here for a holiday. There were always seals loafing around this geo, both in the water or hauled out on rocks, and until that moment I'd have called a bull seal a big animal, but suddenly the seals were small and tender, and they knew exactly what was going on. In the waters of the geo, about sixty feet below us, the seals were mustering quietly, heads held above the waves. I'd expected to see them lolloping up onto rocks in panic, but instead they hung vertical and looked out at the slow, dreadful fins, while the killer whales held their council. With each incoming wave, the congregation of seals rose and fell, and for a long moment all was tense calm.

Then the killer whales moved. They moved so fast, I think I screamed. The females came in two volleys; a few leaps and they were exactly below us, exactly where we'd landed in the dinghy. As soon as she reached the rocks the first animal careened, showing her white belly, and she drew her right flank along the rocks, as though she was glad to feel them, as though she was scratching a maddening sea-itch.

Screaming, jumping up and down at their sheer speed and panache, inside I thought, *She's smelling it*—I thought the huge animal below was smelling a bouquet of rock, seals, vegetation, maybe even us. That's what my human mind said—how she seemed to relish the sensation. Then, with these four animals below us, we heard them blow— all synchronised, a sound low, regular and industrial, like a Victorian machine.

The waves still washed vaguely up against the rocks, and just at the place where water met rock the four killer whales aligned themselves one behind the other, and it seemed to me already, even in my excitement, that there was something peculiar about how I was seeing them. Four killer whales in front of my eyes—big, big, animals—but something about the play of their black-and-white livery was confounding. It was the white patch behind the eye: it seemed to deflect the gaze, the way a mirror or amulet deflects the evil eye.

As I say, I think I screamed, but Jill or Stuart was tugging me, shouting to come on, and we set off running.

The animals had turned west and were moving tight against the island, following its contours. We followed them from above—once again, I was running along a clifftop after killer whales. Again! The same as the year before on Shetland. My friend Tim had been there then. We'd run along a cliff much higher than this; it was Tim who'd pointed out the slow-moving entourage of gannets. That day we'd managed to keep up till we lost the animals in a bright band of glare, but these ones were hard against the rocks, and very much faster, and hell-bent on something. They'd ignored the Poll Thothatom seals, but were moving at terrific speed—hunt speed—cutting through the waves' turquoise backwash, rounding every promontory to the next inlet, out again and into the next.

Hampered by thick grass, our own pounding hearts, we hadn't a cat's chance of keeping up, but it was worth trying, and even when they were out of sight we could hear, coming up from below, like a steam pump in a basement, that thrilling *whomp, whomp.*

What Jill and Stuart and I said or did or called to each other is blown out of my memory, except that we shouted a lot, and ran hard. Every moment we dreaded a sudden thrash and a bloom of blood spreading on the surf: *Keep calm and watch*, I'd told myself—*even if it all gets bloody, try and watch, 'cause you won't see this again*—but abruptly the four killer whales struck away from us, and again, in two-by-two formation, they swam directly across a bay toward the low peninsula of Sceapull, half a mile off.

Now we could catch our breath. Catch our breath and look through binoculars at the four fins slicing through the water, still travelling fast. Somehow the seals over on Sceapull knew the killer whales were in town, because they, too, were gathering in calm groups, until they were visible only as heads above the water, like floating footballs, waiting.

Somehow we understood that these four killer whales were going to loop the whole island, so, figuring they'd round the tip of Sceapull, then drive up the island's west side, the three of us—like spectators at a grand prix—took a shortcut, and pounded up to the crest of the island, then ran pell-mell down its steep north side to where we knew there was another geo, so long it almost cleaves the island in two. From there we'd see the killer whales again as they flashed through.

Acid burn at my sternum, taste of blood, tussocky earth and sky flashing, and my heart pounding; suddenly I was reminded mine was an animal body, all muscle and nerve—and so were they, the killer whales, surging animal bodies, in their black and whites, outclassing us utterly. We timed it well: the animals powered round the headland and into the geo below just as we arrived, sending a couple of eider ducks scuttering away, but the killer whales carried on regardless. Again I had them right in my gaze as they leaped through the water, but again that white behind-the-eye patch threw me. Black and white, it's the conjurer's garb: a moment's bewilderment, a sleight of hand, and you're gone.

By the time we'd run from Poll Thothatom halfway round the island, up over the hill and down the other side, there was no running left in us, and all we could do was jump and shout as the four animals travelled on through the surf zone northward, with the cliff at their right sides, and their vast Atlantic domain to their left. Two by two they went, leaping clear and low over the water, showing the pale underside of their tails as they went down, until at last they were out of sight.

And that was that. We stood for a while, yearning after them, the scary, beautiful animals, as one yearns after a dream, then we turned to head back to the bothy.

Except—we'd forgotten about the male. The male who'd been left behind on his own. Just then I chanced to glance back down at the inlet below us—and there he was. He was rounding the cliff, entering the inlet, conveying his black dorsal fin through the water as if balancing it on a tray, the fin yawing a little as he swam.

This time three of us stood quietly. This was different; a different kind of tension, local and particular. After the females' sheer speed and élan, this animal had an air of solitude about him, as though he'd been holding back, almost out of courtesy, while the females went about business of their own. But now, here he was.

Above us, around us, the summer day carried on oblivious, the helpless waves washed the rocks, fell back again and, beyond the cliff-sided inlet with birds on its ledges, the Atlantic lay to the horizon. All was focused here: one huge predator, cruising at his own speed, nearer to us and nearer. We were looking down from above, and he was heading toward us, his fin cutting through the grey-green water. Gradually, as he neared, the bulk of his body became visible: black and white, rippling under the skin of the water like a spectre. Stuart lifted his camera and I my binoculars, and we focused on that fin. Tugged in close, it was thick and rubbery, but not rubber. It was glossy, a sort of flesh-rubber—and just a little bit crooked. I could hear the clicking of the camera and the waves' wash, and through the binoculars I saw that this fin had the slightest of wavers, a slight S-bend and, as I looked, the voice in my mind said, *I know you*. But right then Jill cried, 'Oh no . . . !', and the thought was dismissed.

Oh no, because also in the geo was a single seal. In our excitement we'd missed her, and she had somehow missed the message every other seal apparently knew. A dreamer, a loner, she was oblivious to the killer whale stealing up behind her because she was facing the wrong way. She was gazing up at us—humans! Up on the rocks! Objects of fascination! Humans who'd run down the hillside pointing and shouting! Who were suddenly bellowing again, 'For God's sake, it's behind you!' as if this were all a pantomime, and a fate could be turned by the wave of a magic wand.

A hundred questions. After they were gone, a hundred questions. As we walked back to the bothy, feeling marooned and elated, we talked about what we'd witnessed. The females had indeed whipped round the entire island: we saw them again heading back down the eastern side, then they'd regrouped with the male, and eventually the whole party left, en famille, heading southwest toward Sula Sgeir.

A hundred questions. A small patch of blue on the hill was the towel I'd dropped; it felt like a long time ago. It was certainly a long time since I'd run so fast my lungs ached, since I'd screamed freely—so much for keeping your head when all around were losing theirs!

We had plenty of wine among our essential supplies, and sat that evening drinking and talking. I recalled how the first animal had rolled, seeming to relish the graze of the rock against her flank. Only then it occurred to me that she wasn't smelling the land at all. Cetaceans can't smell. Not like a dog can. With what would they smell? They may have been only twenty yards away but they inhabited a different sensory world—I'd just made that bit up, out of my own humanness.

There had been no blood. We'd been braced for blood, but none came. Did the seals know that this wasn't a real raid? Could seals decipher the text messages killer whales send between themselves? There were seals aplenty, but the killer whales took none at all, not even the lone dreamer. She had lived to idle another day; the bull killer whale had simply dismissed her, had turned and swam off. A wave of a magic wand.

What then? It was almost as if they were checking an inventory—tearing round, slamming open cupboard doors, taking stock. Or, our best speculation, maybe we'd seen an exercise. Maybe we'd seen two mothers training their young in the Way of the Killer Whale: watch and repeat—like this, like this, like this.

We talked through the evening to no conclusion. Out of the shifting sea, the witless sky, out of the ambivalent world had come terrible certainty: a natural law, laid down in black and white, but mystery, too.

———

Night came, or what passed for night. I couldn't sleep, so I dressed against the cold, crept out and walked down to the ruins. The surf boomed under the cliffs. If the seals were calm again, singing loopy psalms of deliverance, I can't recall. In due course, down at the chapel, the petrels began to arrive. They darted and chased in the night, giving their high chatter, the walls striking sparks of reply. Little dusky things that flit over the ocean, so small you could hold them in the palm of your hand.

———

Cleared of dishes of an evening, the bothy table accumulated notebooks and bird reports, archaeological monographs, plans and photographs. One evening, maybe a week after we'd arrived, Stuart was sitting opposite Jill and me, head bowed, noting figures and tapping a calculator, calibrating the figures his field work was producing. He'd covered about half the island with his tapes. Abruptly he said,

'There's some consistency emerging here. Almost forty per-cent decline, I think, all over. And very suddenly.'

We paused. We all loved the Leach's petrels: their mid-night flit, the backchat they gave us from their burrows.

'That's bad,' said Jill.

'Why, though?' I asked, but Stuart didn't answer.

'Maybe they get eaten . . .' Jill said, but he shook his head. 'I'm sure it's not predators. Bonxies get the blame, but I'm sure it's not just that.'

'What, then?'

Again he shook his head.

'But you must have some idea,' I persisted. 'Is it to do with climate change—with the ocean—is there not enough food . . . ? What do they eat, anyway?'

'Zooplankton, larval-stage fish . . . creepy-crawly things.'

'Plankton? We're not running out of plankton, are we?'

This time Stuart put down his pencil, took off his glasses and pinched his eyes.

'I *don't know*. But something's going on out there.'

Stuart often said there was no such thing as 'natural har-mony'. It was a dynamic. Populations expand, then crash. Mysterious things happen—catastrophic things sometimes, on the island, everywhere. Nothing stays the same.

Our attitude to the village houses we explored and the fields we walked was tempered by a particular piece of knowledge. This: the Rona people hadn't simply quit their tenancy and sailed away to a life less isolated. Neither had they been forcibly cleared. The village was abandoned be-cause the people had died—all wiped out, suddenly.

It happened about 1680. Their fate was discovered because

of a shipwreck. A man called McLeod, his wife and a 'good crew' were heading home from St Kilda to Harris, but a storm blew up which drove them a hundred miles north until they were cast up on the rocks of Rona. They managed to save themselves and some provisions, but their boat was destroyed. They'd have been hoping for help, but what they found were corpses.

What had happened is unsure; the stories are peculiar. A plague of rats had somehow swarmed ashore and devoured the people's supplies. Pirates had stolen their bull. No boat had come north from Lewis that year, which might have brought supplies. These calamities, compounded, were too much. But, with everyone dead, who was left to bear witness?

The shipwrecked party buried the bodies, and overwintered; then, in spring, fashioned a new boat, which they sailed home to Harris, to arrive like revenants. That was then. No one has really lived on Rona since.

———————

On our next to last day, Jill said to Stuart and me, 'Come and look at this stonework.'

She led us down through the ruined village to its southern edge, then toward some more curved low walls, built, as were all the dwelling houses, of stone and turf. To my untrained eye these walls looked no different to the others, but Jill beckoned us to follow her.

Then she jumped down into a curving sort of trench. There, she knelt at the entrance of a short passageway about four feet long. She brushed the side wall with her hand. Its stones were close-packed and neat.

'See how different this stonework is to the rest, how thick? This wall's about three foot thick. Solid. But now, come and look here.'

From the doorway, she followed the external wall a few yards rightward, to a place where it had partially collapsed. There was a hole just big enough to peer into. She handed over her torch and told us to look through the gap. It was like spying through a letterbox into a hallway beyond.

'It's hollow!'

'Caved in, I think.'

She took the torch herself and shone the light into the gap within the wall, so the light played along a particular stone, which was tilted with one end in the earth.

'See that stone? If that's a lintel, and if all that stuff that looks like a floor is actually accumulation debris, then we're looking at a passageway enclosed within two walls. Now, come up here . . . ?'

She climbed nimbly up onto the wall-head and stood above us on an uneven platform of flat stones.

'This is its roof, a bit caved in . . .'

'You're standing on the roof?'

'. . . of a cell-like structure. Which is a side chamber to that bigger interior, the one that first passageway entered into. This chamber is contained within the thickness of the wall. Maybe it was a sleeping area. All of this'—she gestured around her—'was a very thick-walled circular structure.'

'That means it's old?'

'Oooh, two thousand years? But what's happened is that new people have come and changed it to suit themselves. So, jump down here again, come inside . . . and you have a rectangular room, cut into the pre-existing round structure, see? This was done much, much later . . . Look how the stonework here's not very well made, really, compared to where we just were?'

'Two thousand years? You mean, when the Christians came, there was already a thousand years of settlement?'

Jill smiled. 'Could have been people here, or they could have come and gone . . . more than once.'

'Long periods of abandonment . . .'

'Maybe centuries . . .'

'Perhaps that's what this is,' I said, meaning that perhaps someday in the future, when unimaginable change has come to the life we know, a few acres far out in the Atlantic might be pressed into service again.

———

Many people, including the Stornoway coastguard, knew we were on Rona, but nonetheless, as we cleared the bothy on our last morning and prepared to leave, we all three kept glancing at the horizon. Nothing was said, but only when the boat appeared, a steady gleam in the southeast, did we relax. When it did appear, that was our signal to move. The skipper wouldn't want to hang about, so we began to heave all the seabags, sleeping bags, gas bottles, tape recorders and notebooks back down the hillside to the geo, where black rocks tilted to the waves.

Seals were basking there again—they'd watched us come, they'd watch us go, but the rocks we stepped from were different now. They had a wild glamour about them, as though sprayed with an invisible graffiti tag: *'Killer whale was here'*.

Those killer whales. Perhaps the eye has a memory of its own. One day, a few weeks after we'd returned from Rona, when the sense of light and spaciousness was beginning to wane, an email arrived from a biologist called Andy Foote.

Dr Foote worked then with the North Atlantic Killer Whale ID project, which was based at Aberdeen University. Out of interest and a sort of public-spiritedness, we'd sent him photographs of the Rona animals. By magnifying the pictures and by comparing nicks and scars on their fins and backs with pictures held in stock, Dr Foote concluded that, yes, this party of killer whales was the very same five as had often been seen around Shetland the previous summer. When, from the cliffs of Noss, I'd watched a fin appear out of the water, what I'd seen was a puzzling, six-foot, slightly crooked black line, as if, as I thought then, someone had drawn a stroke with a pencil. A year and 180 miles separated the two encounters, but when, on Rona, I'd focused the binoculars again on a stately, slightly wonky fin, and thought hello, chances are it was indeed the self-same animal.

Dr Foote wrote: 'This is only the second set of photos of this party of killer whales on the west coast of Scotland, so it's a useful bit of data.'

A bit of data to him, but to me it felt like an initiation. 'Believe what you see,' say the eye-trained naturalists. Aye, right. Most of the time you'll sound like a idiot. But once in a blue moon you might be right. You just might be making the same journeys as these other creatures, all of us alive at the same time on the same planet.

Tonight, at home, with the blinds closed against the winter dark, the shipping forecast gives '. . . increasing severe gale force nine later'. But that's nothing. Some storm waves are so big they sweep clean over the peninsula of Fianius.

I'd like to witness that. To see Rona in winter, just for a few short days; to hear the sea roar and spend long nights under the wheel of the stars. You'd soon know why the houses were dug down deep into the earth.

The seals will be there, but the birds will be flown. The Leach's petrels, new colonisers of the village, will be away far down into the Southern Atlantic. The cliffs will be bare, too, the puffins and guillemots dispersed out to sea. Skuas likewise, all headed south. As for the crossbills, heaven knows. One day, and with one mind, they must simply up sticks and go, twittering over the waves.

THE STORM PETREL

———

WE FOUND IT ON RONA, the very day we'd arrived, and in keeping it maybe I imagined I could bring home something of the sky and spaciousness of that island, at least for a while.

It wasn't the dead bird we saw, lying on the turf, not at first, but a tiny wink of metal. I said, 'Look, what's that?' and Stuart replied, 'Storm petrel. They breed here. But ringed—that's a real find.'

So here it is on my desk, in a polythene sample bag. An ex-storm petrel, just a clump of desiccated feather and bone, with a tiny ring on its hooked-up leg. When you report a ringed bird it's called a 'recovery', but this one was beyond hope of that.

My five-volume wartime *Handbook to British Birds* says that storm petrels are 'essentially pelagic'; they 'never occur inland except as storm-driven waifs'. That's the kind of language they inspire. There's a lovely poem by Richard Murphy, called 'Stormpetrel,' which begins: 'Gipsy of the sea / In winter wambling over scurvy whaleroads / Jooking in the wake of ships . . .'

At only six inches long, dark brown with a white rump, somewhat like a house martin, you'd think storm petrels too small to jook anywhere at all, never mind in storms, but they manage fine, and come ashore only to breed, in crannies between stones, on islands and cliffs at the ocean's edge.

So the bird is small and the ring on its leg even smaller. Back at the bothy we had to peer at it down the wrong end of binoculars, to make out the number and this terse address. 'British Museum, London S.W.7.'

The rings on other birds, bigger birds, gulls and suchlike, often have space for the word 'inform'. 'Inform British Museum', they say, which makes it sound as though the bird in question had transgressed somehow, had jumped parole. The 'inform' makes the bird-ringing project sound imperious and Edwardian, which it was—Edwardian, anyway, because bird ringing began in 1909. But the storm petrel's leg is so twig-thin, there is no room for an 'inform'.

A few days after we got home I did contact the British Museum, via its website. There are boxes to fill in:

Ring number: 2333551

Type of bird (if known) Storm petrel.

Sex of bird (if known) Unknown.

Age of bird (if known) Unknown.

Was the bird dead or alive? Dead.

Recently (one week)? Long dead. Desiccated corpse.

What had happened to the bird (hit by a car, oiled, etc.) Possibly predated.

Where found? Scotland. Island of North Rona.

Where, more precisely? The north-pointing peninsula called Fianuis.

When found? Early July.

I pressed 'submit', and the form went off on its own mysterious flight, leaving me with the questions not asked:

Smell of bird?—mysterious, musky, like an unguent.

Where found, even more precisely? Under an earth-fast rock, on a patch of gravel, almost at the point where the vegetation expires altogether, and the waves pound ashore.

What kind of day? A lively, companionable summer's afternoon, with a sun bright enough to glint on a tiny metal bead, and make us notice it, the only man-made object in all that place.

———————

It was the twentieth century before it was ascertained that birds do actually migrate; it seemed so improbable that swallows, for example, flew all the way to southern Africa. They obviously vanished in autumn and reappeared in late spring, but some folks thought they just hid, or hibernated in the bottom of ponds. Gilbert White frets around the subject of migration; he hedges his bets. When he was writing this letter of 1769, all options were open:

> 'When I used to rise in a morning last autumn, and see the swallows and martins clustering on the chimnies and thatch of the neighbouring cottages, I could not help being touched with a secret delight, mixed with some degree of mortification: with delight, to observe with how much ardour and punctuality those poor little birds obeyed the strong impulse towards migration, or hiding, imprinted on their minds by their great Creator; and with some degree of mortification, when I reflected that, after all our pains and enquiries, we are yet not quite certain to what regions they do migrate; and are still farther embarrassed to find some do not actually migrate at all.'

'Hybernaculum' is his word for the winter quarters a swallow repairs to, but where was this hybernaculum? His other words were interesting, too. 'Embarrassment' and 'mortification' almost suggest that the Enlightenment just then dawning, all that science and discovery, might have been driven not by the will to master and possess nature, but out of chagrin. As human beings, our ignorance was beginning to shame us, because we didn't know the least things, like where swallows went in winter.

The British Museum passes the forms on to The British Trust for Ornithology, who organise bird-ringing in the UK. So in due course a computer printout arrived from the BTO. It informed me that the storm petrel had been ringed twenty-four years previously, not on Rona, where we'd found it, but 170 miles northeast of there, on the island of Yell.

Yell—I knew that place. It's one of the northernmost Shetland Islands. Only the summer before I'd been there with my friend Tim. We'd seen killer whales off the cliffs at Noss, and made a road trip north via the chain of ferries, passing farms and small towns and the oil terminal at Sullom Voe. We'd traversed Yell, then taken another ferry to the farther island of Unst and made our way to see the gannetry at Muckle Flugga.

All that was one place, stored in one corner in my mind, but Rona was wholly different. Different direction, different culture: uninhabited, remote and Hebridean. As soon as I read the letter, though, a connection shot between them. Suddenly they were linked by a flight-path, straight as an arrow. I thought I knew my maps, but not as the storm petrel does.

Perhaps if you were some sort of purist, if you carried a torch for 'the wild' and believed in a pristine natural world over and beyond us, you might consider it an intrusion to catch a bird, and make it wear a ring or a tag. Perhaps you'd consider that their man-made burden violates them in a way. I admit there was something uncomfortable about the metal ring, soldiering on while the bird's corpse withered. But when I got the chart out, traced the route, measured the distance, and understood that yes, of course, on a southwest bearing, you could swoop via certain channels from the North Sea through to the Atlantic, on small dark wings, it was because this one ringed bird had extended my imagination. The ring showed only that it was wedded to the sea and, if anything, the scale of its journeyings made it seem even wilder than before.

It was ringing which proved that swallows indeed flew south, and did not stupefy in the bottom of ponds, and ringing, too, which showed that storm petrels do the same. They migrate from Shetland or Rona or their many other breeding places, down to the vast pelagic hybernaculum off Namibia and South Africa. A few come to grief; become small, washed-up bodies on a faraway shore, some bearing a return address. An address! Ludicrous thing for a storm petrel to carry. 'The Ocean' would be their address, save for those weeks when they're obliged to creep between stones to breed.

So that's why I keep the bird's remains, here in this room, my own hybernaculum—if only for a while. It's just a tuft of feathers in a polythene bag, a tiny skull, and with that silvery ring above its shrunken, black webbed foot. I keep it for the intimacy, and for the petrel smell: fusty, musky, suggestive of a distant island in summer. And I keep it out of sheer respect because, in life, this ounce of a bird had made twenty-four return trips the length of the Atlantic. Twenty-four at least—which is not bad at all, for a waif, wambling.

VOYAGER, CHIEF

———

Voyager, chief of the pelagic world,
you brought with you the myth
of another country, dimly remembered

—STANLEY KUNITZ

SOME TIME AGO, long before I'd discovered the Hvalsalen in Bergen Museum, I found the vertebra of a whale. It was on the low turf of an uninhabited Hebridean island, just up from the beach. It was perfectly bleached, and some yellow sea pansies had taken advantage of the shelter it afforded; they bloomed within the oval where the spinal cord would have passed.

Finders keepers. I dare say the pansies had first claim but I picked up the bone anyway, intending to carry it home, a splendid thing, part anatomy, part sculpture. I still have it, and from it all my interest in whalebones developed. It's not big; more than likely it had belonged to a minke, which are small as whales go. It's about fifteen inches across at its widest, but heavy, like an engine part, with three smooth, propeller-like vanes emanating from a oval hub and, above the solid hub, the hole, diameter of my forearm.

To get home, the bone and I had to cross Glasgow by subway. It was strapped to the outside of my rucksack—or I was strapped to it. That amused me—being lashed to a portion of whale, diving from the traffic-loud street down escalators into the tunnels below. It's in my attic room now, a sign of the pelagic world.

I suppose I'd always half known that there is a whale presence in these islands. Or, put the whale's way, these islands are a surprising, sometimes disastrous presence in the sea. Since I found my own bone, I'd began to keep an eye out for whalebones deposited around the landscape. I mean, erected there deliberately, not just washed up. I'd kept an eye out in private houses and gardens or, occasionally, in old-fashioned small town museums. I'd begun to notice that around the sea's edge, and surprisingly far inland, there are whale relics: melancholy beautiful bones.

In the centre of Edinburgh, for example, at the park called the Meadows, there stand the jawbones of two great baleen whales, set upright to form a double arch. They're in a poor state now. Mouldered and corroded after a long century of chimney and exhaust fumes, they're much the same texture and same drab colour as the trunks of the nearby trees whose branches overshadow them. They vault over a footpath popular with students and workers on their way downtown—heading to the office through the jaws of the Leviathan—but although the footpath is called Jawbone Walk, the bones are pretty much ignored. One way to make people look at them is to stand there looking yourself, but you soon feel idiotic, and maybe folk are right to disregard them; they're just city curios, a bit of Victorian Gothic, like angels on tombstones. Except—they're not stone. They're real, animal, anatomical, announcements of the natural.

There's the story (of course, there's always a story) of how these huge bones came to be stranded in a city park, out of sight of the sea—it concerns girls, and knitting, but such stories are not the whole story. The whales' own narratives are unrecorded, but given that these bones date from Victorian times, the whale stories don't take much guessing.

The human side of the story is this: the jawbones have been in Edinburgh since 1886, when they arrived south from the Shetland islands to form part of a great exhibition—the International Exhibition of Science, Art and Industry. For six months the flat grassy Meadows were filled with the confidence of Empire, with grand halls and bandstands. There were trams, and life-size model houses, and demonstrations of the latest technologies: mining, sugar-refining, paper-making.

There were 'Women's Industries', too, glove-making for example, and a show of Shetland and Fair Isle knitting. This is what the whalebones were for: the Shetlanders had brought them along to form the structure for their stall. (A 'picturesque tent', one reporter called it.) Under this canopy young women from the islands gave demonstrations of knitting. Relays of girls sailed south, six at a time, 'buxom, sun-browned, modest-looking', and they sat in their stall and knitted all day. One photograph survives. It's in the Shetland museum, and it shows the girls and their chaperone seated at their work while over their heads the whales' jawbones rear in a pointed arch, swagged and veiled with fishing nets and flags and shawls.

To citified visitors, the whole ensemble must have spoken of 'northern-ness', of whales and fish and crofts and spinning. An idealised vision, of course. Their chaperone sports a ridiculous hat, but the girls are all bare-headed, with their hair neatly drawn back, and they wear white aprons and long thick skirts. The girls are lovely, but it's the ghost presence of the whales which is arresting, both in the photograph and today, for real, in the Meadows, with no drapery, and with buses and pedestrians passing by. As for the animals, well, they went up in the chimneys of the nineteenth century. Science, Art and Industry, all of it smoothed and lit by whale oil.

———————

The whales whose blubber was rendered into oil came in those days mostly from the Arctic. From almost every east coast port, ships sailed north to the waters around Greenland, Jan Mayen, Spitzbergen. They sailed from Hull and Whitby, Dundee, Aberdeen, Peterhead.

William Scoresby was a Whitby man, who, even by the time he enrolled at Edinburgh University in 1806, was already the veteran of several Arctic whaling seasons. He had to leave his classes before the end of spring term to join the ship commanded by his father, William senior. By the age of twenty-one, the younger Scoresby had his own command, but to him whale-catching was a necessary chore. He was much more interested in the science of the Arctic. Among much else he made drawings of the shapes of snowflakes—hitherto unknown; he conducted experiments with magnetism, and surveyed the east coast of Greenland. When whales were sighted and he was obliged to break from his surveying and give the command to chase, this was an irritation.

Because of Scoresby, the headlands and inlets of the Greenlandic coast read like a roll call of the post-Enlightenment; from Cape Barclay in the south to Cape Bright in the north, the ice-capped peninsulas and ice-choked fjords are a long list of male grandees: as he put it, '. . . respected friends, to whom I was wishful to pay a compliment that might possibly survive the lapse of ages'. Every fjord and island is for a friend or admired superior, the largest fjord of all, named in honour of his father, is Scoresbysund.

From those waters, thousands of whales were brought back to Whitby—to all the whaling ports—reduced to bone and blubber packed in barrels. They caught polar bears, too. Scoresby once brought a live polar bear home, and dispatched it to Edinburgh as a gift to geologist Robert Jameson, his tutor there. It lived out its days in a 'commodious den'. A bleak Greenlandic peninsula is still called Jamesonland.

In fact, in the town of Scoresbysund, now renamed Ittoqqortoormiit in the East Greenland language, there is a church, bright with gleaming brass and colour after the snow and leaden skies outside. From the ceiling of this church hangs a wonderful votive ship, with all the masts and rigging, and the name on its stern is Baffin, which was Scoresby's vessel.

Knowing all this, I'd expected that Whitby's whale arch would be an ancient relic, linking the town with the waters around Greenland. I imagined the arch might even be one of those Scoresby himself had brought back—to signal a successful trip the whalers mounted a jawbone against the mast, so it would be visible to those waiting ashore. Certainly, Whitby's arch is as celebrated as Edinburgh's is ignored. It stands on a rocky scarp above the harbour. It stands, that is to say, in front of the grand white-painted hotels and above the amusement arcades and ice-cream stalls and the 'Dracula Experience' and the picturesque tent of Gypsy Lee, who, if you are feeling fear, or uncertainty, will help you by gazing into her crystal ball.

But climb from the harbour, and you'll discover that Whitby's jawbone arch is actually brand new. Slender and pale, the jaw's sides rise like the arms of a ballet dancer, and it frames a view across the harbour to the skeletal ruins of Whitby Abbey, high on their own clifftop opposite— ruined stone arches framed within an arch of bone. Turn a little and what it frames is the grey and depleted North Sea.

It was a May day, Whitby was as thronged as ever with holidaymakers; a huge gang of bikers had roared into town. I spent a few minutes sitting on one of the many benches beside the whale ach looking down at the harbour, where an old lifeboat, all trigged out in bunting, was making a little trip.

Folk strolled out along the harbour walls. A man puffing on a pipe sat beside me and we fell into conversation. He said, 'This town lives on its past. Trades on it. Without the past it would be nothing.' He said, 'If I could travel back in time, just for a day, I'd go back two hundred years to the docks here . . . it would be fantastic to see all the sailing ships, and all the different people . . .'

'When it was a whaling port?'

'. . . Aw, the smell!'

Much was pastiche, but amid that the whale jawbone we sat next to was entirely real. It attracted attention in a much more subtle way than the amusement arcades did; no bells and flashing lights, it just stood there. I watched as one man came along to the whale arch and carefully photographed it, very close focus, looking at the smooth texture of the bone, and the long groove and tunnel which, I presume, had once carried an artery. When the photographer had left, a woman came by, and she stroked the jawbone with her hand, looking wonderingly up to its apex. Perhaps she was trying to imagine the creature alive, a creature whose jaws were double her own height. After all, this is as close as many people will come to an encounter with a great whale.

The Edinburgh jawbones are, I believe, from fin whales. Fin whales occur all over the world. Whitby's is a bowhead, which are found only in the Arctic. In Scoresby's times whalers called bowheads the 'right whale'—the right whale to hunt. For that, for being the 'right' whale, bowheads suffered terrible exploitation; their numbers are now reckoned to be just one hundredth of what they were before European whalers hoved into view. They are protected now, of course, but Alaskan Eskimos are licensed to hunt a quota of bowheads each year. A board beside Whitby's arch explains that the jawbone was a gift from the people of Alaska. It was flown over from Anchorage and received with all due Yorkshire pomp and ceremony, and unveiled by Miss Alaska herself. It was given to replace an older arch, which had likewise been a gift—that one from the king of Norway, but which had weathered away. This is strange, this gifting of whalebones between nations. Whale jaws and pandas.

From the whaling grounds east of Greenland, the ships pushed farther and farther west as they killed and killed the whales. The first lighthouses—mere gleams in the dark— were built partly, ironically, to protect the lucrative whaling fleet, and were themselves fuelled by whale oil.

Not all whale parts have such elaborate or known histories as the Edinburgh or Whitby ones. Not all come from whales slaughtered. Sometimes whales strand, as we know, or wash up already dead. If you travel as far north as Caithness by the A9, which by then is pretty well the only road, you'll find another jawbone. It overarches a field gate on the seaward side of the road. I suspect it came from a whale washed up, because there are no port towns nearby, but there are low cliffs and steep-sided geos. Neither are there office workers here to pass beneath it as in Edinburgh, or picture postcards or beauty queens as in Whitby. Grasses grow at its base; it's been there a long time, and is now held in place by wires, so someone's keeping an eye on it—and because of this concern, there's something venerable about it, in the same way that an ancient yew tree seems venerable.

Carry on further northwards, and when you reach the coast you'll see, a couple of miles out in the tidewrought Pentland Firth, the low, green island of Stroma.

No one lives on Stroma now. From the mainland you can make out derelict croft houses, their kale-yards all gone to nettles. Despite that—or maybe because of it—the island has a carefree atmosphere. Sheep graze; the otherwise empty houses and hearths are knee-deep in sheep dung. When the last families quit for the mainland, certain things were left behind, understandably. There's an enormous iron mangle at a gable end, and a broken cart, sinking into the peat, and a red phone box and, propped against a drystone wall, a huge whale's vertebra. Mottled and mossy now, it looks like a piece of classical statuary, a winged male torso.

I found it by chance on a visit to that island, and took a photograph. Though it was a bright May afternoon, with the thrift in bloom, and terns screaking overhead, in the photo the whalebones turned out silvery, otherworldly, as though moonlit.

———

The more you find of these relics, the more you look at them, indoors or out, the more they seem imbued with a particular presence. Whatever it is, a whale arch is not a tri-umphal arch; these are not trophies. All these bones, regard-less of the species, share a solemnity and slightly luminous quality. We're now in the Northern Isles, Orkney and Shet-land, places with a long connection to whaling. In times past, large schools of pilot whales came by these islands, and if they were sighted everyone ran to their small boats to ca' the whales; that is, drive them ashore to be killed for meat and oil. But this is big whale country, too; humpbacks are sighted annually, fin and sperm whales on occasion.

At Sumburgh Head on Shetland, beside the car park that serves the lighthouse, where the cries and smell of guillemots reach you from the cliffs below, there stands the back of the skull of a sperm whale. It is as broad as it's high and slightly curved, like a fragment of a chariot. Sheep treat it as a scratching post; there are always tufts of fleece adhering to it. Keep walking up onto the headland and, just before the white-painted wall of the lighthouse, the more delicate, streamlined skull of a minke whale lies along the ground.

Of all the whale jaws I know of, the most majestic and unsettling is found not on the Northern Isles, but the island of Lewis. To travel across that island, east to west, is to cross an apparently empty landscape. Miles of undulating brown green peat-moor lie under a huge Atlantic sky, with the hills of Harris rising to the south. In summer, polythene sacks filled with newly cut peats wait at the roadside to be taken home. After crossing the moor, you reach the township of Bragar, where crofts and houses straggle loosely along the coast, and beyond that, on a clear day, you can see the Flannan Isles, and beyond them, the open Atlantic.

It's an unlikely place, being so domestic, but by one of these houses, a modern bungalow just few yards from the road, in a garden of long grasses and leggy blue geraniums, and accessed by a little garden gate, almost, if one can say this on Protestant Lewis, like a wayside shrine, is mounted the jawbone of a blue whale, and it is just monumental. Bound by iron hoops onto the ends of two stone walls, it's twenty foot high, and deeper than my own arm is long, but still with a tapering elegance. It comes with a terrible story—a whale's story.

In about 1920 the animal was sighted just offshore, already dead. It had died of wounds. An explosive harpoon which had been fired into the animal had failed to detonate, the whale had broken free of its captors and swum on, trailing fifty fathoms of rope, the harpoon head bitten into its flesh. At length it succumbed. Where it had come from, no one knew, but blue whales and fin whales were hunted off the Scottish coast then. A Norwegian-owned whaling station operated on Harris; its chimney and slipway still stand.

Even now, the whale is not free of the wretched harpoon: the four-barbed head hangs like a pendulum from the jaw's apex, where it swings a little in the wind. Swings in the wind. Despite the bungalow and the little garden gate and the flowers, the whole affair has a feel of the gallows.

Of course, every whale relic represents a disaster for that individual animal, a death, a wreck, a stranding, a slaughter, and something of that atmosphere cleaves to their bones. But there's something else, something about the whale. Maybe its just the scale that makes them appear to us as near mythic; part mammal, part architectural, inhabitants of an imagined otherworld. There's a kind of whale-inspired religiosity which must have suited the Victorian mind— whalebone corsets and religiosity. Toads were said to have a jewel in their heads; render down a whale and what do you find but the arch of a church door. (Even Scoresby quit whaling in his thirties to take the cloth and become, in due course, vicar of Bradford.)

By chance, I found Whitby's old whale jawbones, the ones replaced by the Alaskans, housed within another relic—the decommissioned church which is now the town's

Heritage Centre; the bones were leaning across the arched west window. Recently, too, I learned that there is a jaw-bone arch—or part of one—within the grounds of Glastonbury Abbey. Far from the ocean, the whale in hallowed ground, in the heart of Albion.

But we're in the North. Orkney and Shetland were where the whalers put in to take on crew and water before heading for the ice; Scoresby sent last letters home from Baltasound and Lerwick. It's where they paid off those crewmen again. If they'd been trapped in the ice and obliged to overwinter, they came home in a pitiful state. The Orkney harbour town of Stromness had its own scurvy hospital. (Sometimes the crewmen didn't return at all—Franklin's ships *Erebus* and *Terror* put in at Stromness to take on water, before sailing on to seek a Northwest Passage. They were last sighted by two whalers, entering Lancaster Sound and oblivion.)

I mention Stromness in particular because, of all the whale relics I've come across in recent years, a favourite is in that town, and it's easily the smallest. It's tucked quietly into the town museum, one of those nineteenth-century troves, established by Literary and Philosophical Societies, which still retain their cabinet-of-curiosities feel; replete with objects which haven't been filtered and 'interpreted' for us, and which remain rich places to spend a rainy afternoon. (Whitby also has a glorious Lit-and-Phil museum—maybe it's a phenomenon of seaports, and the intrepid Victorian age.)

At Stromness, there are the ghastly instruments common to whaling ports: flensing blades and lances, and the frame of an umbrella made of baleen, and a sperm-whale tooth etched with the image of a little whaleboat being snapped in two by a vast sperm whale, and tiny sailors plummeting into the sea. This was a favourite scrimshaw subject. William Scoresby himself drew such a scene—a little whaleboat tossed on high by a lash of a whale's tail, as though the fight with the whale was a fair fight. That, of course, was before the invention of the exploding harpoon.

The museum stands on its own little pier; its small windows look out onto the water. Upstairs are old stuffed bird skins in cases, various mammals, a turtle mounted on the wall and, in one particular case, a small assembly of objects that have defied categorisation. The careful taxonomy which has held among the birds and birds' eggs and pinned-down butterflies has here failed, and these last things are grouped together because they share some quality—in this instance, roundness. It's the kind of arrangement a little girl would make. There's a neat pile of striped snail shells and, next to that, a coconut which washed up long ago on some Orkney shore and, next to that, three smooth brown pebbles, which are not pebbles: one is cut open so you can see it's actually made of hair—'Hair balls from cows' stomachs', says the label. And next to the hair balls is something shaped like an open purse, the size of your cupped hands. It's thick but hollow, and wrapped over on itself, with one lip tucked under the other, leaving a fissure. It is a vessel made of the densest bone, and is smoothed and rounded as though it had rolled in the ocean for a long time. Because of the gap, it is somewhat like a mouth. However, it wasn't made for speaking, but for listening. The label reads, 'Whale's ear drum'.

These eardrums were prized. I've heard it said that, being strong to withstand great sub-sea pressures, they were the only things to emerge from the final furnace the whales' carcasses were put through—the left-over bits that is. I've read—frankly, I've read as much as I can bear about whaling—how the whalemen slithered and groped in the whale-gore, seeking these eardrums. They took them home as keepsakes, fancying they could hear the sea in them, or whale song. Sometimes, though, they're grotesque. Some whalemen painted the eardrums—there are two in Shetland got up as Punch and Judy—but mostly they are left plain, and sit quietly around the coast. As well as Stromness, there are whale eardrums that I know of in Aberdeen and Lerwick and Scalloway, and who knows how many in private houses. I find them beautiful and sad and complete; all that can be said about sea-waves and sound waves, song and utterance, is rolled together in these forms.

The Stromness one is grey and old, and as you look at it lying on its shelf you have to wonder. What did it hear, in life? Across what distances? Whales apparently hear through their jawbones; they have no external ears as we do—so the very jawbones now raised around the country at large would, in life, have picked up sound waves in the ocean. What did they hear, these jaws, these eardrums? They heard us coming, that's what.

———

How, these days, do you acquire a whale relic? Well, I suppose you could apply to the Eskimos of Alaska, but whales do die naturally, at sea, though we find that hard to comprehend, having killed so many ourselves. They've been living and dying long before humans set sail in pursuit of them with harpoons.

Some years ago a fin whale washed up dead on the Scottish island of Coll. Every time a big whale washes up, even dead, a minor pandemonium ensues. In times past it would have been a bonanza—the bones would have been sprinted away for roof trusses; meat to carve up and eat; blubber for lamp oil. This time, the National Museum of Scotland laid claim to the carcass, as an 'important addition to their collection', and sent a truck over on the ferry to collect it. However, certain of the islanders had other ideas. Before the lorry arrived, someone removed the jaws and hid them—rumour says they were buried in the sand dunes. The islanders wanted them for an arch. An argument ensued, the museum prevailed, and one of the islanders said, plaintively, 'It seems everything disappears, and we have nothing to remember the whale.' I think she meant, 'Everything disappears into a vault in a museum'; but this is another meaning to the whale arch, to whale relics, which that woman discerned— something elegiac. Such has been our violence toward these animals that we sense in a jawbone arch a memorial not just to that particular whale, but almost to whalehood itself.

Almost, but not yet. What else did the whales hear, with their huge eardrums? They heard a sea change. The beginnings of deliverance. They'd have heard, felt, the drill bits biting into the seabeds, oil tankers sliding over the surface above, signalling a development in human technology.

The whales heard the twentieth century come and go. And, though there are whaling nations still, and we're not quite out of the woods yet (I'm thinking of Stewart's Park in Aberdeen, where a broken whale jaw stands among the leafy trees), I suggest that if they cared to listen, if we could indeed whisper into those eardrums, they'd hear something, at least in this country, like atonement. Which brings us to the strange case of North Berwick.

North Berwick is another pleasant seaside town. It sits at the southern side of the Firth of Forth, on an agricultural plain. Just inland of the town, however, there rises an abrupt, green cone of a hill called Berwick Law. It's a long extinct volcano and, at 600 feet, quite a landmark, announcing to seafarers the entrance to the Firth. There had been a whale arch—or a succession of them—on its summit for 300 years. A wonderful place for one, high up in the weather, in view of the sea. But the weather did what weather does: the last arch was recently deemed 'unsafe' and, one day, a few years ago, it was taken away.

The people of North Berwick missed their whale arch, and they got together and one thing led to another and now Berwick Law is again surmounted by a jawbone arch. Except—it's not. It's not plundered from a washed-up whale nor supplied by Alaskans or anyone else. You toil up the grassy hill to the summit and, with the North Sea to the east and the hills of Fife to the north, there is the whalebone arch. It's surrounded by a railing, you can just reach through and touch it, but when you do, it feels like . . . plastic. What they've installed on Berwick Law is not a whale's jaw but a fibreglass replica.

I don't know what to make of this. Was it a principled decision not to source a real whale's jaw? Certainly. And yet, and yet . . .

I'd climb a hill to see a real whale's jawbone. I'd take the kids, have them measure themselves against it and notice how the sun and salt wind has worn and changed it, transforming what was once alive. I'd like to view it against the sea's horizon, note how it pulls animal body, land and sea together in one huge stitch. As I say, in the presence of a whalebone you look at the sea differently and, because attitudes have changed, you look out, always in the secret hope that there might be living whales out there, which one day might appear.

A fibreglass replica. No doubt this is right and good. But you have to wonder, standing on the hilltop at Berwick, if this is how it must be. If we are adjusting our relationship with these greatest of animals, and with the non-human world as a whole, if we're now, at last, refusing to slaughter or torture any more whales, does it mean that when we do reach out for the natural, in wonder or shame or excitement or greed, what we must touch is a man-made substitute?

––––––––––––

Aside from the Stromness eardrum, the whale relic I visit whenever I can isn't a jawbone arch, and therefore not festooned with meanings. It's not even very big. Again, it's on the Orkney Islands, the northwest side of the Orkney mainland. There, near the Brough of Birsay (as good a place as any for spotting minke whales) where the land trends eastward, a narrow path follows the coast. It's an elemental place in any season—loud waves surge between long skerries; eider ducks ride the waves and, often, seals watch you as you walk. Look ahead though, and you'll see beside the path what you might think is some huge bird, perched on a pole, hunching its wings to lift away, or even a standing stone, but it is, again, the vertebra of a whale. I don't know what kind. The vertebra is mounted about five foot high on a curved stalk which looks like wood but is a rib from the same long-dead, presumably washed-up animal. I like it for its shape, its graveyard air of mystery, and, because the bone is so greyed and porous now, it's hard to say if it's bone at all. I like it because it's not intended as a symbol, has no story that I know or wish to know, no knitting or harpoons or interpretation boards or fibreglass. Someone's raised it, part homage, part joke, but in the end it's just a whalebone, anatomical and mortal, and set to face the wide sea, whence, of course, it came.

WIND

————

IN ALMOST A FORTNIGHT the wind had barely eased, although it was May. The days were long but they felt dark and wintery because of the gales. Gales by day, gales howling through the short nights. If there was a lull the silence was uncanny, tentative. Sure enough, it meant only that the wind was crouched behind the horizon, shifting a notch or two before it rose again.

It was said, that when Hirta was inhabited, a thorough-going gale would leave the people deaf for days.

We could go outdoors, being careful to close the inner door of the house before opening the outer, else there was all sorts of banging and damage. Someone had rigged an old ship's hawser to hang on to as you crept up the external stair to the upper storey. A recent innovation; in the olden days the houses had no upper storey. We slept up there, and the wind carried on through the night. Only once did I wake at dawn and hear a wren singing. Every other dawn there was the wind.

Depending on its direction, you could work out which places were unwise to visit—which cliff tops were best avoided, which slopes might be too exposed. Glen Mor was safest; it faced west, so the wind was onshore. We went there several days in a row, getting clouted properly as we crossed the hill to reach it. All the time the sea roared. A burn runs down the glen and, where it spills over the cliff, the wind would catch it and send up plumes of rainbow.

I recall no sense of the warmth and expansiveness of Maytime—just a feeling of being embattled, of shouting, of being overdressed. I discovered that gusts of 70 mph can knock me down. The sensation is not of being tumbled like a leaf, but of being thumped by an invisible pillow. It doesn't hurt if you've lots of clothes on; one just finds oneself on one's knees, as if beholding a miracle.

On one of these outings we came across a whooper swan which had died en route to its summer grounds in the Arctic. Visible from some distance away, a white rag on the bright green turf, it was lying with its neck extended and its yellow beak pointing north like a way sign. On some impulse we opened its wing, its right wing, and held it outstretched. It was astonishing: a full metre of gleaming quartz-white, a white cascade. You could understand at once how these creatures make the journeys they do; its wing had been formed under the wind's tutelage, formed by and for the wind.

But we are not creatures of the wind; we were frayed and weather-worn. In every outing, every conversation, every plan, the wind had to be admitted and negotiated with, or discussed behind its back, like a teenager who'd gone off the rails.

We left the swan and walked on up toward the ridge, and from there further up to the communications mast, which shrieked as the wind passed through it. From that vantage point—we sheltered in the lee of some sort of hut—the sea all around was grey-green and crazed, driving against the cliffs. It was wildly dramatic but the screaming of the mast soon became unbearable.

Of course there were no boats, had been none for days, and would be none till the wind died and the swell calmed, whenever that might be. So a doubt crept in—when would we be able to leave? Certainly not on the day intended. Maybe not for a while.

But this is the modern world, at least for now. A helicopter comes out twice a week to serve the radar base. It brings personnel on for their stint, and takes away those going on leave. We discovered there might be spare places on Wednesday's flight; if we packed ourselves up and put ourselves on standby we might get on. But Wednesday's was cancelled, leaving us with a negated feeling, all packed and nowhere to go.

The Thursday was dismal, wind of course, and rain too. The hills were dreary, the ground saturated. Starlings, caught in the blast, dashed by the window. However, the helicopter was on its way. Though the wind was strong, it was funneling downhill from the west, and that was alright. Were it blowing in eastward from the bay, it might have capsized the helicopter as it lifted off.

In a concrete shed we zipped each other into yellow survival suits, then strapped on life-jackets. Already wind-deafened, we were given earplugs and then we made our way against the wind across the asphalt. Instructed by hand-signals how and when, we moved, doubled over, across the helipad and into the machine.

I'd never been in a helicopter before. It yawned into the air without my realising. Like a bird it could swap the state of being on land with that of being airborne by a mere alteration of attitude. Then we were chugging over the sea. The crossing, hours by boat even nowadays, took twenty-five minutes. Small windows at foot level showed the sea below as the swan would have seen it on its last flight, migrating in its family group. If they ever look down.

There are myths and fragments which suggest that the sea that we were flying over was once land. Once upon a time, and not so long ago, it was a forest with trees, but the sea rose and covered it over. The wind and sea. Everything else is provisional. A wing's beat and it's gone.

ACKNOWLEDGMENTS

Many people made this book possible, giving of their time and knowledge with forbearance and goodwill. I'm grateful to Professor Frank Carey and Professor Stewart Fleming, both of Ninewells Hospital Dundee; to Dr Alison Sheridan of the National Museum of Scotland; to Dr Terje Livseland and Dr Anne Karin Hufthammer of Bergen Natural History Museum; and to Prof Gordon Turner Walker and the 'whale team' of conservationists. My thanks also to Ian Parker, Strat Halliday, Adam Welfare, Angela Gannon, and James Hepher (all of the Royal Commission on the Ancient and Historical Monuments of Scotland) for memorable trips to St Kilda, and to Susan Bain of the National Trust for Scotland, for allowing me to join them.

Thanks to Tim Dee for the birds, Peter Dorward for the caves, and boatmen Donald Wilkie, Bob Theakston, Norman Tenby, and Angus Campbell for happy landings— and for getting us off again. I'm especially grateful to Stuart Murray and Jill Harden, island-goers in chief.

Shona Swanson, Meaghan Delahunt and Susan Sellars were there when things got tough.

Peter Dyer and Henry Iles made a mere typescript into a beautiful artifact, which Nikky Twyman copy-edited and proofed. Nat Jansz continues to be an editor of uncommon insight and patience. Again I thank her and Mark Ellingham for their constancy and hospitality.

Love to Phil, Duncan and Freya Butler, as ever.

PERMISSIONS

Lines quoted on p. 71 from "Landscape With the Fall of Icarus" by William Carlos Williams, from *The Collected Poems: Volume Two, 1939–1962* © 1962 William Carlos Williams. Reprinted by arrangement with New Directions Publishing Corp.

Lines quoted on p. 117 from "The Knapsack Notebook" by Matsuo Basho, from *Narrow Road to the Interior and Other Writings*, translated by Sam Hamill. © 1998 by Sam Hamill. Reprinted by arrangement with The Permissions Company, Inc., on behalf of Shambhala Publications Inc., Boston, MA.

Lines quoted on p. 207–208 from "Stormpetrel" by Richard Murphy, from *The Pleasure Ground: Poems 1952–2012* (Bloodaxe Books, 2013) © 2013 Richard Murphy.

Lines quoted on p. 215 from "The Wellfleet Whale" © 1985 by Stanley Kunitz, from *The Collected Poems* by Stanley Kunitz. Reprinted by arrangement with W.W. Norton & Co.

PHOTO CREDITS

Preliminary pages (p. v front) Lichen © Kathleen Jamie; (p. viii, opposite) cabinet containing a whale's eardrum, Stromness Museum, Orkney © Alistair Peebles.

Aurora (p. x) View through a ship's window © Kathleen Jamie.

Pathologies (p. 20) *Giardia* organisms in a biopsy of the small intestine © Professor Frank Carey.

The Woman in the Field (p. 42) top: The author, 1979 © Kathleen Jamie; bottom: Cist burial, North Mains, Strathallan © Historic Scotland.

The Gannetry (p. 70) Gannets © Stuart Murray.

Light (p. 86) Light through branches © Janet Hayton.

Hvalsalen (p. 90) Hvalsalen, Bergen Museum © Zina Fihl/ Bergen Museum; (p. 95) Hvalsalen, Bergen Museum © Kathleen Jamie.

Moon (p. 116) Moon behind tree © Henry Iles.

Three Ways of Looking at St Kilda (p. 126) Boat at St Kilda; (p. 132) St Kilda prefabs with derelict cottages in background © Stuart Murray; (p. 140) Surveying St Kilda © Jill Harden.

La Cueva (p. 160) La Cueva de la Pileta © Mojo Appleton.

Magpie Moth (p. 168) Magpie moth © Niall Benvie/naturepl.com.

On Rona (p. 174) Aerial view of Rona © Stuart Murray; (p. 196) killer whales circling Rona © Strat Halliday.

The Storm Petrel (p. 206) Storm petrel © Tomas Svensson; (p. 213) ring © Phil Butler.

Voyager, Chief (p. 214) Whalebone on Lewis © Stuart Murray.

Wind (p. 234) Helicopter © Heary/iStockphoto.

Final page Whale fin © Stuart Murray.

ABOUT THE AUTHOR

KATHLEEN JAMIE was born in the west of Scotland in 1962. She studied philosophy at Edinburgh University and at nineteen she won the prestigious Eric Gregory Award, which enabled her to travel. At twenty she published her first poetry collection, *Black Spiders*. She is a regular contributor to the *Guardian* and BBC Radio and her nonfiction writing and poetry has appeared in *The New Yorker*, *Orion*, *Poetry*, *The Economist's Intelligent Life*, *New Statesman*, *Boston Review,* and the *London Review of Books*.

Her poetry collections to date include *Selected Poems; The Bonniest Companie,* which won the 2016 Saltire Society Book of the Year Award; *The Tree House*, which won both the Forward prize and the Scottish Book of the Year Award; *Jizzen*, which won the Geoffey Faber Memorial Award; *Mr and Mrs Scotland are Dead*, which was shortlisted for the 2003 Griffin Prize; and *The Overhaul*, which won the 2012 Costa Poetry Award and was shortlisted for the T. S. Eliot Prize. She has also won the Somerset Maugham Award, a Paul Hamlyn Award, a Creative Scotland Award, and the 2017 Royal Geographic Society's Ness Award "for outstanding creative writing at the confluence of travel, nature, and culture."

Her first nonfiction book, *Among Muslims,* was described as "utterly luminous" by the *Independent* and "one of the most powerful accounts by a contemporary Western writer" by the *Times Literary Supplement.* Her subsequent collection of prose essays, *Findings*, is considered a landmark in nature writing. Her essay collection *Surfacing* is her most recent work.

Kathleen Jamie is a professor of creative writing at the University of Stirling, and lives with her family in Fife, Scotland.

KathleenJamie.com